QUESTIONING TECHNIQUES

Artur Kaiser was born in Germany in 1943. His university training included psychology, sociology and the development of teaching methods. After working as instructor and training leader with the Porsche Company and various computer programming groups, he established, in 1970, a management and education consultancy at Oberstenfeld, near Stuttgart.

In addition to training teachers, group leaders, sales people and staff from all levels of management, his bureau coordinates with scientific and industrial experts on a wide variety of specialized projects. The author now serves as an independent adviser to various West German organizations, including the television network ZDF, the German Railway, Allianz Life Insurance Company and the Porsche Company. He also lectures regularly to teachers' and journalists' associations, trade unions and schools.

Dr. Kaiser has written three books in German, of which this work and *Motivation Techniques* (Druck erzeugt Gegendruck) appear in English. He is part of a new orientation in business/education counseling, and applies the insights of modern psychology to solving communication problems on a direct and practical level.

Artur Kaiser

QUESTIONING
TECHNIQUES

 = Hunter House

Originally published in German under the title
Fragetechnik: richtig fragen, mehr erfahren
by Deutsche Verlags-Anstalt GmbH, Stuttgart
© 1977 Deutsche Verlags-Anstalt GmbH, Stuttgart

Authorised translation by Norbert M Lechelt and Ullah Marten
© 1979 Servire BV, Netherlands

First U.K. edition published in 1979 by Momenta Publishing Ltd.
                                        23 East Street, Farnham
                                        Surrey GU9 7SD

ISBN 0.86164.103.5

First U.S. edition published in 1979 by Hunter House Inc. Publishers
                                        748 East Bonita Ave.
                                        Suite 105
                                        Pomona, California 91767

ISBN 0.89793.001.0
Library of Congress Catalog Card Number: 78-70616

Cover design by Qalagraphia

Set in 11 on 13 point Baskerville Roman and Italic on AKI Automix

Printed and Bound in the USA by El Camino Press
                              La Verne, California.

CONTENTS

1. Dialogues 1

2. The conversation partner as receiver of
   our questions 7

3. Intention *versus* willingness 15

4. Question-types: building blocks of questioning
   dialogue 23

5. A well-formulated question is half the answer 35

6. The function of questions and the use of
   questioning techniques 41

7. Personnel interviews 47

8. The teaching conversation .63

9. The oral examination 79

10. The sales conversation 83

11. The consultation 93

12. Question time! Talk shows and journalistic
    interviews 101

    Fields of application of questioning techniques . . .107
    Analysis of a sales conversation 108-109
    Tables for analysis of practice examples 110-115

    BIBLIOGRAPHY 117

1

DIALOGUES

'If you ask a lot of questions, you get a lot of answers.'

Do you think your ability to obtain agreement in a conversation depends on the questions you ask or on the arguments you use?

This question gives a choice of alternatives and is formulated in a neutral fashion. But when the same question is considered in the context of a book entitled 'Questioning Techniques', it takes on a suggestive tone. The question is also clumsy; its formulation does not allow sufficient freedom for the development of a dialogue. Generally, a dialogue only reaches agreement when both participants have good arguments at hand which they play out through skillful use of questions. It is not important which of the two verbalizes the convincing argument. When one conversation partner arrives at the other's idea in response to a question, that is a successful questioning dialogue.

Questioning dialogue involves a form of questioning that is adapted to the purpose, situation or context of the question and the conversation partner. The four basic characteristics are:
— the questioner is assumed to have an intention;
— the questioner assumes that the conversation partner possesses the knowledge required and the ability to express it;
— the questioner formulates the question in such a way as to stimulate the desired response; the question is judged 'suc-

cessful' if the response fulfills the questioner's expectations, in other words if he is satisfied with the answer.[1]
— Willingness to answer 'correctly and honestly' is not a prerequisite and varies with the questioning situation.

'What you have to say about questioning dialogue is very interesting, but you can't always ask questions!'
(Now you can argue or continue questioning.)
'Have you ever experienced conversations where it is not possible to ask questions?'
'In a sales interview, surely the prospective buyer only wants to know the advantages of the product?'
(Continue *directive* questioning.)
'Does the prospective buyer want to know all the advantages of the product or only some of them?'
'Only those which interest him.'
'How do you know which advantages interest him?'
'By asking him what he needs the product for, etc.'

The understanding reached here through the use of open and directive questions could possibly have been reached through an argument, but conversations consisting only of arguments are really an exchange of blows and, without your being aware of it, lead to confrontation.

'Doesn't your experience show that it is difficult to reach agreement in a confrontation?'

Don't be annoyed by the suggestive tone of that confirmation question! This type of question should only be used after the facts have been presented in order to establish a sort of running balance.

According to our definition, questions are requests in the form of interrogative sentences or impulses that stimulate a meaning-

ful verbal reaction in order to gain information. This information includes the following:
— facts unknown to the questioner;
— opinions of the conversation partner;
— indications about the conversation partner's ability or competence;
— a desired statement from the conversation partner.

In the simplest case, questions are immediately recognizable as requests for information. The following questions seek facts and opinions which the questioner can only learn from his conversation partner.

'Where does it hurt?' (Doctor)
'What do you expect from your job?' (Personnel officer)
'How do you keep informed about beauty-care?' (Cosmetician)
'What are your interests?' (Careers advisor)
'What do you think caused this dispute?' (Industrial psychologist)
'What are your short-term goals?' (Management consultant)

The conversation partner's responses are also an indication of whether he follows or knows what's going on.
Is the following sentence a statement or a question?

Associate: 'I only want to know why you didn't tell me about it.'

Grammatically speaking, this sentence consists of a statement (I want to know) and a question (why didn't you tell me about it?).
Does the cosmetician want to learn something with the following question?

'So you are not satisfied with the cosmetics you have been using?'

Although suggestive, this question is supposed to find out whether there is agreement on this point, after which the ques-

3

tioner can follow-up with a description of the advantages of her own products. In the widest sense, such agreements and approvals are opinions. Similarly the opinions, ideas, ambitions, experiences, points of view and prejudices of celebrities are much sought after by hosts of television talk shows and by journalists as news for their audience. For example:

'And could you just ignore what was happening around you?'
'How do you see the outcome of this election?'
'Would you see victory as a reward or as a challenge?'

The following type of question could be asked by a patient to a doctor, a customer to a salesman, a teacher to his students, or by an examiner to his candidates (in which case you can assume he already knows the answer).

'What do you conclude from these symptoms?'
'How does this motor work?'

An examiner, however, wants to find out whether the candidate knows anything, or how much he knows. It's a bit like the old joke about the Wild West where Jim and Joe are riding across the prairie with a stranger they met a few hours earlier. Joe asks the stranger, 'What is two times two?' The stranger: 'Five'. Joe shoots him dead. An hour later Jim asks Joe, 'Why?' Joe: 'He knew too much!' Only by putting questions and assignments to his candidates can an examiner find out what he wants to know. Therefore, examination questions are also real questions.

Different techniques of questioning may employ open questions, directive questions, alternative questions, suggestive questions and confirmation questions. The type of question you ask is determined by its purpose, form and content, which are based upon the desire to receive a satisfactory answer.

What answer would you expect to the following question?

'How high is Mt. Everest?'

Obviously the answer is so many feet. Does that make it a request rather than a question? No, because it leaves the option open for the answer, 'I don't know.' It is therefore a combination of focused and specific information questions.

By means of another formulation preceding the real question, a questioner can gauge the knowledge of his partner and whether he is willing to communicate it.

'Can you tell me how high Mt. Everest is?'
If yes, then: 'How high is it?'
If no, then end of question.

Alternatively the questioner can provoke his partner into taking a position by expressing his desire to know something with formulations such as:

'I just want to know . . .'
'Nobody can tell me . . .'
'It's a pity nobody knows . . .'

The tone of the questioner's reaction to the partner's response is also useful to elicit more information. For example:

'So?'   'Really?!'   'And?'
'Aha!'   'You don't say!'

Strictly speaking, these reactions are not questions but can be considered as such; therefore they are called *question impulses*. It is necessary to distinguish these clearly from requests, orders or obvious statements (such as, 'Tell me, please,'; 'Pass the bread'; 'Don't talk back, you're coming tomorrow morning at 8!') because the pressure to comply (or not) is much weaker here. Question and impulse both operate on a verbal level, seeking information and appealing for verbal reaction. The strength of this appeal does not depend on the question itself but on the relationship between the conversation partners.

REFERENCE

1. Weidenmann, 'Fragen' in 'Reden und reden lassen', Stuttgart, 1975.

2

THE CONVERSATION PARTNER
AS RECEIVER
OF OUR QUESTIONS

'I hear what I want to hear and not what you say.'

Questioning an unskilled worker is not the same thing as questioning a personnel director — their different vocabularies, modes of expression (concrete or more abstract), opinions and level of education require a different approach.

The obvious requirement of all questioning — so obvious that many questioners don't even think about it and are therefore unsuccessful — is that the question has to be heard, listened to and understood. We don't even need to look at foreign languages and dialects to see that this is not always the case. Just imagine the following situation. The boss has called a worker into his office — something has gone wrong.

'Mr. Jansen, the Quality Control Report shows that 1,000 alarm-clock cases have been incorrectly punched on your press . . .'

This statement is enough to cause a storm of fears and anxiety in Mr. Jansen. His only thought is, 'How can I get out of this?' He is looking for plausible excuses or explanations why it is beyond his responsibility and so he is only listening with one ear (he only hears the words in italics.)

'. . . the edges of the pieces are uneven and from talking to the head of *Quality Control* I hear that they cannot *be corrected. What do you think* is the cause of this *disaster?*'

Mr. Jansen: 'But if they can be corrected, what do you mean disaster? Even Quality Control says it's OK!'

With a background of tension in the relationship, the worker would possibly continue:

'And why all this fuss? You're always looking for an excuse to jump on me. I know you're after me but I refuse to take it any more. I'm going to get the union onto this. What an insult!'

With a background of mutual trust, the worker would possibly continue:

'I'm glad everything worked out all right this time. Well, I'll do some overtime to make up for it. Is Saturday OK?'

From your own experience with misunderstandings, you know very well that we see or hear only what is important to us at the time. If we are involved with planning our garden we become strongly aware of front gardens, or if we are thinking about employing new personnel the newspaper advertisements catch our eye even though we are not consciously looking for them. In other words, our unconscious selection of what we see or hear depends on our motives. The same thing is true of our conversation partner. In addition, there is our background of expectations — are we only expecting a negative response from our superior? Does he symbolize our bad conscience?

What is your past experience of these situations? Did you generally find a practical solution or did a solution just occur?

Let's consider how the worker will react to the situation in the above example. What is his past experience? What are his expectations? Will he immediately feel threatened and become defensive? Does he accept our description of the problem and its effects? Does he suspect negative manipulation? Does he always look for a hidden trap behind any question?

What our conversation partner actually hears, or chooses to hear, depends firstly on his motives, expectations, experience and the background to the conversation. Secondly, what our partner hears or receives depends on the formulation of the question, its content and the way in which it is perceived. Perception, as well as the willingness to perceive, play an important role in the technique of asking questions.

In employment interviews, sales interviews, consultations, journalist interviews and criminal interrogations, the conversation is our first encounter with the partner. Only rarely do we know him beforehand. Nevertheless, we have to form an opinion rapidly in order to select the appropriate questioning technique. Usually we rely on our first impression of appearance, looks, presentation (posture, gesture, facial expressions), voice and choice of words. Surprisingly enough, our first impression of a total stranger is generally informative, unambiguous and subjectively convincing. As a rule, the 'first impression' consists of four characteristic types of response:
(1) affective judgement — 'a likeable person';
(2) personality assessment — 'not so bright';
(3) conclusion from symptoms — 'the bitter line of his mouth shows he's suffered a lot';
(4) recollection of a similar person — 'she reminds me of my gym teacher'.

Should I mistakenly conclude that my partner is not so bright, I will formulate simple questions that may even be stupid. And the conversation partner? He becomes angry because he guesses at my opinion of him and feels undermined in his self-image. Anger leads to a rejection of the questioner or at least to a rejection of what is asked. On the contrary, should I over-estimate my partner and formulate a question that is too difficult, he will not understand me, or will misinterpret me, and I will receive an inadequate answer.

With a conversation partner who is not very likeable or open, we avoid using words which might be interpreted negatively. The questions are formulated more carefully, hinting only slightly at our own particular point of view. Whereas when we trust a likeable person — maybe too much and often without knowing it — we charge our questions with suggestive elements exposing our own opinions and expectations so that we can react positively to our partner. An incorrect first impression can thus jeopardize the success of our questioning strategy.

Experience shows that a person is a better judge of character of someone similar to himself. The more life experience, intelligence, scope and insight into his own personality, as well as artistic ability, a person has, the more accurate his first impression will be. Character traits which manifest themselves through different types of behaviour such as spontaneity and inhibition, emotional responsiveness and apathy, dominance and submissiveness, the degree of inner balance and realness, are usually, although not necessarily, judged more accurately than aptitudes and value-systems. Common errors occurring in the evaluation of a conversation partner are the following tendencies:
— to oversimplify (halo effect);
— to approximate to an 'average' standard (central tendency);
— to project our own unconscious faults and 'hang-ups' onto the other.

The more accurate our first impression, the more likely it is that our questions will successfully find their target.

In short: The way in which a question is received depends on the perception of the partner as well as on our formulation of the question. This formulation in turn takes into account our image of the partner which often derives from our first impression.

'Do you still make love regularly with your wife?'
'How much did you drink last night?'

Would you accept these questions from just anyone? Hardly. The first question would be acceptable from your divorce lawyer, doctor or psychologist, the second from your doctor or cosmetician. Who asks what questions and to whom is controlled in most cultures, though in a vague and inexplicit way. The right to ask questions and the obligation to reply are related to definitions of role. A question about size and kind of corsets can only come from a corset saleswoman. If she then asks you about your drinking habits or your bank account, she will get a puzzled look or a rebuke in reply. A doctor can ask you questions about the most intimate functioning of your body or the secrets of your psyche inasmuch as they are connected to the state of your health, but questions which have no such connection, though they may be less personal (e.g. political or religious attitudes), will not necessarily meet with a willing response.

In short: We are willing to give information when it coincides with our interests.

When we have a problem, we look for a conversation with a problem solver such as a counselor, doctor, social worker, priest or sales clerk. We provide these problem solvers with all the information asked for and which we consider necessary to bring about a solution. If you want to buy a simple product from among the many offered on the market, you will not understand why the salesman asks you where it is to be used and how frequently. However, if the product you wish to buy is more complex or even part of a system, then you will regard the salesman primarily as a consultant with the right to ask questions. Of course, the consultant has to prove his competence by his credentials or by his appearance and his advice.

If you ask a question having nothing to do with your role as cosmetician, such as:

'How much money can you afford to spend on cosmetics?'

you will be refused the right to ask the question with:

'That's none of your business!'
'What's it to you?'
'I don't ask you . . .'

The implication of the following answers is not the same in that the right to question is accepted but an answer is refused:

'I prefer to keep that to myself . . .'
'I really don't know . . .'
'I don't want to talk about it.'

It is useful for anyone connected with sales or distribution to be accepted as a consultant because this role enables him to question as a means of arguing and recommending towards a specific goal. A consultant who exploits this possibility for manipulation, failing to consider the interests of his conversation partner, will have short-lived success with the role.

Skillful questioning technique therefore begins with structuring the initial questioning situation. By taking the more positive role, you are allowed a wider range of questions and are trusted in advance. This in turn increases the partner's willingness to answer. The role of consultant gives you more control over the course of the conversation, facilitates questioning and thus contributes to the success of the conversation.

Of similar importance is the image of his newspaper or media for the journalist and the image of the institute for the interviewer ('university' may sound better than 'Dr. Mayer's Market Research Bureau'.)

When questioning groups, the questions are aimed at everyone, in so far as the formulation appropriate for one member may be invalid for another. Guesses have to be made about expectations, experience and motives. To put it simply: you cannot diagnose individually in a group situation. During discussions and other group activities, you can address individuals directly. You can also focus on an individual in a group situation but it then becomes a dialogue within the context of a group.

If you are interested in taking independent statements from group members as a basis for clarification/assessment or influencing, the following technique may be used (developed by Metaplan, Quickborn). Each group member writes down answers to questions on small white cards (postcard size). Every card has one answer. The cards are then placed on a pin or magnetic board and sorted out. The pattern of recurring answers forms the basis of the assessment.

Where the objective is to influence group behaviour, this technique is seen only as a means of initiating the group process (opinion leader, sub-groups, group standards, differentiation of roles within the group etc.). The follow-up methods are discussion technique, conference technique and case studies.

3

INTENTION VERSUS WILLINGNESS

'I want to sock it to you—but you have to give me an excuse for doing it!'

Whether you watch the latest crime thriller or a court hearing, you will notice that answers to questions don't always come easily. On the other hand, the interviewer who meets up with a frustrated housewife thinks himself lucky when the conversation only lasts twice the intended time — she is so willing to answer in detail.

Willingness to answer questions varies greatly, ranging from complete openness to stony silence. We may distinguish three types of response, each of which requires a different questioning technique.

1. No resistance, because the information does not seem disadvantageous to the questionee. For example questions concerning technical points, professional information or printed information from a public relations department;
2. Actively desired, as it offers the opportunity to express one's own wishes or needs, to talk about one's past performance or similar achievements;
3. Resistance. For example as a result of intentions which run counter to the aims of the questionee, or an unwillingness to talk about one's own negligence or mistakes.

Willingness to respond by giving information varies with the question, even where it exists in principle.

'Yes, I was very interested in this television interview but I don't think I could reply honestly to the question about my sex life.'

Willingness to respond honestly depends, on the one hand, upon the amount of personal involvement and, on the other hand, on whether the assumed purpose of the information runs counter to the questionee's interests.

If the personnel director asks the department head his opinion of one of his group leaders, Mr. Korn, who has always had a good reputation, and the department head doesn't know the purpose of the question, the following thoughts could be incorporated in his answer.

'Now the boss wants to know about Korn's performance as group leader in the current situation. Have I judged Korn too well? I have to stick to my opinion, no matter what, otherwise it will reflect negatively on my ability to judge and therefore on my leadership. If I praise Korn, I am indirectly praising myself as I supervise and direct him. Anyway, if I do anything else I could be criticized. I have to make it clear always that nothing could work without me. Maybe I can get something out of it for Korn. That could help me quite a bit in the next tight situation.'

Suppose the personnel director wants to promote Korn and is gathering information to back up his decision. Here he will receive biased information, which bias he is not in a position to take into account because he doesn't know the department head's motives. It would be simpler if he asked the department head two consecutive questions:

'I would like to hear your opinion of how Mr. Korn has performed as group leader in the two years he has held this position.'
'And now I would be interested in hearing what you think of his ability

to fill the post of head of warehouse administration which has become vacant.'

Excessive praise in response to the second question could mean 'praising him away' whereas not enough praise could mean 'wanting to keep him'. Thus by exposing the purpose of the question you are in a position to take account of the probable motives of the questionee in your evaluation of his answer.

If you are really interested in an answer, you reveal the purpose of your question. However, when a politician wants to lead his opponent into making a particular statement, the purpose is not explicitly stated. The questioner can then assign all kinds of intentions to the question which can be quite uncomfortable for the questionee. It is therefore important for the questionee to ask the purpose of the question. Both in a consultation and in a learning situation, the goal is clearly pre-stated and operationally formulated.

The questioning situation is something of a Trojan horse, as every question contains within it the request for an answer and even no answer is, in a sense, an answer. For example:
— when a doctor remains silent about his patient's condition;
— when an accused remains silent;
— when a worker remains silent to questions about why he wants to resign;
— when a salesman ignores the objections of the buyer.
Every silence is interpreted in this sense: the person being questioned wants to be honest but at the same time he doesn't want to disclose what he knows or intends to do. The questioner's intention will be interpreted as altruistic or egotistic, depending upon the content of the question.

If silence is interpreted as tacit agreement or compromise bringing disadvantages, then it is only human and understandable that the questionee will try to avoid the request the question contains within it in other ways. Every questioner should be aware of the techniques most commonly employed. Rather than outright refusal to answer a particular question, side-stepping, distracting or simply lying will be used. A special method is the counter question: 'Why does that interest you?', which can lead to questioning *ad absurdum* as in the anecdote where someone is asked in a discussion: 'Why do you always answer with another question?' and gives the reply: 'Why shouldn't I?' Another avoidance tactic consists in playing down the meaning of the answer:

'It's not important at all',

or denying one's competence:

'I don't really know for sure . . .'
'I can only make a guess . . .'.

Alternatively, the question can be diverted by taking a word in it literally:

'But what does that mean?'[1]

A more positive avoidance tactic is to expose the conflict oneself:

'I wouldn't like to be forced into saying something in front of my colleague that I don't want to say, but at the same time I don't want to withhold information important to your work . . .'

What can you do when confronted with such tactics? You can either withdraw, insist (more or less successfully) or try an indirect approach.

Thus whether or not a question leads to its goal depends not only on questioning technique but also on the questionee's willingness and ability to answer. Often a question is not enough, and the development of a conversation can be a help or a hindrance to gathering information, as shown in the following extract from a conversation.

Cosmetician: 'Mrs. Adams, the results of your skin test show that the
(to client)   sides of your face are within the normal range whereas the middle portion tends to be oily. We therefore need to see what we can do about changing the middle portion from oily to dry (Author's note: the opposite, equally undesirable extreme). Besides, the moisture elimination is *bad*.'
Mrs. Adams: 'My God! But if my skin gets dry it will peel and that makes it flake.'
Cosmetician: '*No, no*. That doesn't necessarily come with drying.'
Mrs. Adams: '*No?* But I thought you said from oily to dry?'
Cosmetician: '*I didn't say* from oily to dry, I said into the normal range . . .'

Depending on her personality and temperament, the client could now stick to what she heard and start an argument, give in or ignore the answer. In any case, the words in italics will have a negative influence on the conversation and reduce the client's willingness to provide information.

A similar unconscious mechanism is triggered off in a ballot when you want your proposal to be voted on first. There are always those voters who are indecisive and raise their hands hesitatingly. You may have already noticed how these people will look around to see who is committed to the proposal first and, depending upon whether a strong personality votes for it, also raise their hands. There are usually at least two dominant personalities with divergent opinions in any group.

An underhand tactic which is not uncommon is to select your

weakest opponents (as many as you need to push through your proposal) and wear them down primarily by aiming at their physical resistance. A programme scheduled the evening before till late at night, tiring lectures and tough bargaining over minor issues followed by a rich meal with alcohol will increase the strong drop in productivity normally occurring around 2 p.m. (biorhythmic curve). If, after a quarter-hour-long monotonous discussion, these opponents are shocked out of their slumber with the suggestive question: 'Mr. Miller, do you agree to this solution?', the case is won. To avoid being criticized and admit he wasn't really paying attention, the upright man will answer, 'Oh, yes, yes!', and it's all over.

Such influences play a part in questioning technique and are therefore mentioned.

Here are some hints which should help you to gather information more effectively.

1. Think about what you want to achieve with your conversation. For example, do you want to get rid of your subordinate or keep him? Do you want to be in the right or do you want to sell something? Do you want to be tactful or find out the truth no matter what?
2. First try to get an objective view of the subject, which requires
3. Putting aside your own arguments and defenses or even avoiding them altogether.
4. Repeat interesting points with a questioning intonation;
5. At this stage, don't ask questions which might make the other react defensively;
6. Be patient;
7. Avoid diverting attention, e.g. by asking specific questions;
8. Ask general, broad questions;
9. Encourage your partner to carry on speaking with exclamations such as, 'Yes?', 'Aha!', 'So!', 'Now, really?' etc.

10. Such fill-ins compel the conversation partner to speak, providing him with little or no content or material. Remember that the speaker exposes himself;
11. Listen for information between the lines (maybe the answer is hidden) and try to verify whether your interpretation is correct;
12. Verify your information, possibly provoke your partner, e.g. by threatening his self-confidence or by doubting the answer given;
13. Counter with different interpretations;
14. Always let the other explain every statement;
15. No accusations. Always speak in a factual and, if possible, friendly tone as the normal reaction to accusations is at least defensive, if not dishonest.

All these hints can increase your partner's willingness to communicate as well as the reliability of what is communicated.

REFERENCE

1. Weidenmann, p. 100, *op. cit.*

4

QUESTION-TYPES: BUILDING BLOCKS OF QUESTIONING DIALOGUE

'He who asks, leads.' (Stangl)

Let's get organized. Setting aside the function and the specific purpose or goal of the question, let's see just how much freedom one has in answering a question.

Firstly, there are questions that differ in their formulation. For example:

'How high is the church steeple?'
'Is the church steeple 130 or 165 yards high?'

The first question allows us as many answers as possible, i.e., the answering possibilities are totally open. This question-type is therefore called the *open question*. The partner can reply in whatever form, detail, direction or accuracy he likes, i.e., he defines the precision of his answer. Freedom is maintained. The open question is used when:
— we want our partner to express an unbiased opinion;
— we seek new information;
— complex problems need to be solved;
— we are trying to develop many possibilities;
— we want to motivate our partner to free formulation and expression.

The second question is a *closed question*, as possible answers are already given. This question-type includes predefined alternatives (as above), multiple choice and list questions (as in market research).

Multiple Choice Question

How many grams in a kilogram?
1. 200 g.
2. 250 g.
3. 500 g.
4. 1,000 g.
5. 2,000 g.

List Question

To which professional category do you belong?
— worker
— farm worker
— farmer
— office worker
— civil servant
— independent businessman or tradesman
— free lance/professional

The closed question facilitates communication for the questionee in that he has only to choose one of the given possibilities. This question-type limits the range of answers possible. In contrast to open questions, closed questions require more knowledge (or better guesswork) from the questioner. The results are easier to compare because of the predefined responses which anyone can evaluate. The closed question proves especially useful when:

— short and specific information is required;
— the questionee is reserved or not very articulate;
— checking a set of assumptions by means of a series of specific questions to save time (doctor, police inspector);
— comparable data must be collected as a basis for decisions;
— all alternatives are known and new ones are not expected;
— forcing the conversation partner to make a decision by presenting him with alternatives;
— guiding the conversation in a specific direction.

Thus different formulations of a question give different possibilities.

Both open and closed questions can be asked *indirectly* as shown below.

1. Journalist to political activist:
   'Tell me, what are the basic characteristics that need to be eliminated in human beings so that they perform as you would expect?' (*Open question*)
2. Salesman to customer:
   'Do you want your car in red or metallic blue?' (*Closed question*)

Both questions contain assumptions which are not stated. This question-type is known as an *indirect question*. The person who answers the question as asked automatically consents to the assumptions. 'If Dutschke gives a list of basic characteristics, he consents to an indirect question concerning the shocking idea of 'eliminating' human characteristics, and accepts the term 'basic characteristics' (rather than environmental influences) and the implication that he expects a performance from people.'[1] In the second question, the customer's decision to buy a car is being taken for granted.

Indirect questions thus consist in veiling what you really want to know. The questioner does not want to express his intention openly, fearing that a direct question will make the partner realize the implications of the answer or decision and thus inhibit the desired response.

A customer would probably not agree to buy a car so quickly — if at all — were the question asked directly in this way: 'Do you want to buy this model?' 'If you fail to expose the implications of this question-type and give the desired response, you have been had by the clever questioner.'[2]

Indirect questions are useful when a barrier needs to be overcome (e.g. sale) or when one wants to hear an answer given from a particular perspective (e.g. journalist, politician); however for the interviewer, the consultant, the personnel manager or even the teacher, they are very difficult to interpret. A completely false picture can be obtained, as the following example shows.

Interviewer to female worker:
'What do the girls in your department think of their superior X?'
She: 'They all like him and think he's fantastic.'

One would usually conclude from such a general statement that the questionee shares the opinion of the majority. However, this can be a mistaken conclusion, as shown by the test question that followed:

'And what do you personally think of him?'
'I can't stand him and I'm going to quit my job!'[3]

Indirect questions are advisable in social counseling, where a direct question would bring the conversation partner into conflict with social taboos about income, sexuality or a negative attitude to work.[4]

In addition to open and closed, direct and indirect question-types, the suggestive effect of formulation should be considered. For example:

'*Then* you are *also* of the opinion that . . .'
'This can *only* lead us to the conclusion that . . .'
'You don't see a risk in that, *do you?*'
'Do you *still* beat up your wife?'
'So this brand was accepted by all quality-conscious hair-dressers? *How about you?*'
'*Surely* this is *also* in agreement with your own experience, isn't it?'

With suggestive questions a specific answer is cleverly indicated by the choice of words (e.g. surely, also, besides) that intentionally limits the answering possibilities. Suggestive questions are therefore also known as *directive*. Suggestive influences in questioning can be extremely subtle, such as name-dropping, ignoring other alternatives, one-sided presentation of the pros and cons, appealing to stereotypes (conventional values and prejudices) or generally accepted social values.

The danger in a suggestive question is not always apparent and is usually underestimated, as can be seen from the following example. Mr. Johnson is called to court as a witness because he saw the accused leaving the scene of the crime. During the cross-examination, he is nervous and not fully attentive.

Public Prosecutor: 'So you saw the accused *running out* of the building?'
Johnson: 'Yes.'

The Public Prosecutor's use of the word 'running' gives the jury the impression of a man fleeing, which Mr. Johnson was probably not aware of at the time. For him the question may only mean that the man had left the building.

We use the term 'suggestive effect' when perception, thought or action are guided in a specific direction or when other alternatives are eliminated.

Suggestive questioning is used when:
— the questioner wants to elicit approval of his own opinion from the conversation partner;
— the questioner wants to see how sure the other is of his opinion;
— the questioner wants to overcome mild opposition;
— the questioner wants to turn the conversation in a specific direction or maintain a specific flow;
— the questioner is trying to create a good atmosphere.

A particular form of suggestive questioning is the *rhetorical question* where the questioner does not even wait for the answer. Whether the answer is 'yes' ('Surely you also agree that there should be more peace in the world?') or whether the question is used as a provocation to the contrary ('Should I work myself to death?'), the speaker can always provide the answer himself as it is obvious.

A combination of indirect and suggestive closed questioning is, for example, the tactic employed by the travelling salesman to get an appointment where the first problem arises at the door. You can often build up a very positive self-image in front of a conversation partner. First, consider what positive attributes you can assign your partner that would be both credible and to your advantage. This means that the assigned identity must be composed so that it will lead to the behaviour you are looking for, once your conversation partner has accepted your image of him. You will also have to give him the impression and assurance that he is not being taken advantage of. This is based more on suggestion than indirect questioning.

'Am I speaking to Mr. . . . in person?'
'While enquiring among my circle of colleagues concerning an execu-

tive who knows his profession especially well, your name was mentioned to me. As an executive you are most certainly interested in accurate information about your marketing potentials, aren't you? Of course, you don't want to hold such a discussion standing in the doorway. That's why I would like to arrange an appointment to see you.'
'Is it possible during office hours or would the evening suit you better?
'Today or on the . . .?'
'Immediately after 6.30 p.m. or at 8.00 p.m.?'
'You are also time conscious, which shows the practical approach of a businessman. Surely you don't want to dismiss information without examining it. I'm sure no-one can tell you that black is white, isn't that so?
'When would you like to consider how you can benefit from this?'

Transactional analysis is an important contribution to questioning technique in that it demonstrates that dialogues are essentially conducted on two levels, the overt or verbal level and the covert or psychological level. Here is an example from Eric Berne.[5]

Sales representative: 'This machine is better, but you can't afford it.'
Housewife: 'That's the one I'll take.'

The sales representative states two objective facts: 'This machine is better' and 'you can't afford it'. These facts are aimed at the reasoning faculty of the housewife who should now answer, 'You are right on both counts.' The representative, who is an experienced trickster, aims the hidden psychological arrow at the self-esteem of the housewife. She reacts something like this: 'Regardless of the cost, I'll show this arrogant guy that I can afford as much as his other customers!'

The following example shows a similar process, though perhaps more clearly.

Large formal party.

Young man: 'Are you interested in having a look at that butterfly collection back there?'
Woman: 'Great! When I was a child I used to love looking at collections.'

Arriving in the back room, where there is a butterfly hanging in a display case, he kisses her.

If she consents to a conversation about love games initiated by him then she also allows him to kiss her. She consents to the meaning of his words rather than their literal content. If her reaction is one of rejection, she will take his words at face value and 'literally' expect a butterfly collection. This can also happen to you, — the hidden transaction I mean!

To take an example from a television series:

Boss: 'I realize that Mrs. Lesley is a good worker. She really pulls her weight. But she is difficult. You don't always have it easy with her, I should think.'
Woman worker: 'What can I say to that?'
Boss: 'Don't you find her rather difficult, personally I mean?'
Woman worker: 'I wouldn't put it like that.'
Boss: 'But you don't find her easy-going, do you?'
Woman worker: 'What does *easy-going* really mean?'
Boss: (impatient and leaning over the desk) 'I don't understand why you don't want to tell me what you think. I only want to see Mrs. Lesley in the right light.'

Can you detect the hidden question? The question where the word in a literal sense is of secondary importance?

'What does *easy-going* really mean?'

The boss realizes she isn't interested in a definition of 'easy-going' but that she is trying to avoid giving a straight answer.

Conversations and questions can thus easily contain a double meaning which, if unnoticed, can lead to embarrassing mis-understandings. Nor can one react directly to the implicit meaning. Think of the impression our young woman of the butterfly example would make if she replied, 'I am not interested in your advances.' The questioner could reply that she read something into his question that wasn't there at all. Therefore the reaction takes place on the same level: 'Oh, well. You know butterflies never interested me.'

Questions where the contents are of secondary importance are also found in greeting rituals or conversations about the weather — at which the English are the proverbial masters. A lot of questioning goes on without really telling you anything.

Hidden questions are mostly concerned with social taboos which could meet with indignation and rejection were they openly expressed. The reason for this is that the relationship or role play which allows such a question is built up slowly (like the role of a lover or a colleague in whom one confides about the boss) or cannot be built up at all because it would be incompatible with another existing role (co-worker of the boss).

Two specific forms of hidden question are occasionally used in social research:

a) the error-choice technique, where only misinformation is given within the form of a closed question.

'Does Germany have 1 million or 7 million foreign workers?'

Depending upon the choice of answer, the interviewer will be able to detect the social attitude of the questioned (too low, does not notice foreign workers and therefore has no aversion).

b) the information test, i.e. the interviewer is simply testing factual knowledge. This strategy is based on the observations of empirical psychologists that the more a person knows about a subject, the more interested and involved he is in it. His interest increases in proportion to his knowledge. A person doesn't usually start learning about something unless he is interested in it.[6]

There are numerous ways to maintain the double meaning within a dialogue, the most usual being learnt from personal experience and the psychological tricks and mechanisms communicated by books or films. One way of creating distance from this and checking the direction of the conversation is to ask a question about definitions.

'What do you mean by . . ?'

Another way to create double meaning is through the use of images and words which though once understood on a simple level now point in the direction of a taboo.

'Would you fancy a ride in the countryside?'

spoken to a woman, or:

'Would you like to see the architecture of the barn?'

These questions also retain an element of safety in that the questioner has the possibility of dropping the double meaning without losing face. The precondition of hidden questions is being able to assume that the partner has understood the double meaning and interprets the question on a psychological as well as literal level.

While hidden questions relate to other levels or totally different themes that are not made explicit, indirect questions operate on the same level and with the same theme, though without mentioning certain assumptions related to the content of the question.

The selection of the appropriate question-type and its use help you to reach the desired goal of your questioning. When and in which sequence to use specific question-types cannot be stated in a single rule as these choices depend on the purpose of the question and the course of the conversation. An interrogation and a sales interview are simply two different pairs of shoes.

REFERENCES

1. Weidenmann, *op. cit.* p. 109.
2. *Ibid.*
3. Neuberger, O.: 'Das Mitarbeitergespräch', 1973.
4. Schraml, W.: 'Das psychodiagnostische Gespräch', Handbuch der Psychologie, Volume 6, 1964.
5. Berne, E.: 'Games People Play', 1964.
6. Neuberger, O. *op. cit.* p. 132.

5

A
WELL-FORMULATED QUESTION
IS HALF THE ANSWER

Social research has clearly shown that the formulation of a question influences the results of a study. This is especially important in voting, public opinion polls, referendums, in court proceedings or anywhere where the choice of words or syntax used can lead to bias or confirmation of a favoured opinion.

The following test, conducted in our group, shows the effect of formulation as 11%.

Formulation 1
Do you think the U.S.A. will join the war before it is over?

Formulation 2
Do you think the U.S.A. will be able to keep out of the war?

Results
yes: 41%
no: 33%
don't know: 26%

Results
no: 30%
yes: 44%
don't know: 26%

(Note that the positive attitude to war in formulation 1 is expressed by: yes = 41%, and in formulation 2 by: no = 30%.)

Thus the first requirement is the use of neutral words which are not open to misinterpretation. For example, 'woman' instead of 'lady', 'dog' instead of 'animal', 'car' instead of 'vehicle'. Avoid at all costs subjective expressions of expectation such as:

keep out of/join before it is over

may we hope/do we have to fear.

Concerning the formulation of the question, the following criteria should be taken into account:

1. Does the question start with a question word? For example, who, what, where, why, when, how, etc. or with a verb, for example, are we, has he, does she;

2. Is the question goal-oriented? Does it aim at the desired information? (e.g. 'What can we do in this situation?' instead of 'Is there nothing that can be done?' when you want ideas for dealing with a situation.)

3. Are the concepts used ambiguous? For example, as a response to the question, 'How do you class these societies?' (economically or sociologically?) the answer 'Rather good' can mean 'Adequate' or 'Not so good' depending on the standards of the speaker.

4. Is the question short?
Personnel manager to warehouse worker: 'Why did you drop that box?' instead of 'With what intention did you impulsively decide to drop that box filled with valuable electronic components from a height of 6 feet?'
(Admittedly that's exaggerated, but similarly complicated expressions are not so rare.)

5. How understandable is the question?
Teacher to pupils: 'How do you judge the relation between social relationships and population in communities such as hamlets, villages, towns and cities?' Too abstract.
Management trainer to factory foremen: 'How would you describe in terms of your experience the reciprocity of positive feedback and worker productivity?'

6. Is the question appropriate?

   This can be related to the persons being questioned in terms of their experience, intelligence, attitudes and their relationship to the questioner, as well as the actual questioning situation. Imagine walking in on a small argument between a married couple over his weekly football-game-and-drinking-night, asking: 'Come on, Joe. How come you're not ready yet? The game starts in an hour!'

7. Are you asking more than one question?

   E.g., 'I would like to know how you justify your decision', 'Have you considered the financial aspect?', 'Didn't you have other possibilities?' Here the questionee does not know where to start as each question is aimed at a different aspect. The question is thus confusing.

Short, understandable and direct questions are generally clear and accurate and so we don't need to discuss them separately!

The social scientist René König suggests the following guide lines in his book, 'The Interview', as an aid to receiving unbiased answers.

'In an interview concerning a subject which the person questioned is not particularly familiar with or lacks the necessary technical jargon for, it is sometimes better to preface questions with a descriptive introduction that sets up a frame of reference. The question itself can then be quite short.'

Either explain all the alternatives involved in answering your question or none at all. For example, if you ask: 'Are you giving promotions in your company based on achievement?', often the answer 'Yes' will come too quickly without considering the fact the sometimes promotions are given for reasons of seniority, personal favour, etc. If the interviewer reminds the questionee of other possibilities, he will get a more thought-out answer. For certain purposes, it may be preferable not to mention other alternatives or possibilities.

For example: 'What is the main criterion for promotion in your office?'

It is frequently helpful to ask questions related to the immediate experience of the questionee rather than questions of a general nature. For example in a leadership study the interviewer asked: 'Think back to the last time one of your employees was late for work. What did you say?'

König gives reliable advice on how to reduce defense mechanisms against delicate subject areas to a minimum: '. . . suggest that others hold as well the opinions one would normally treat with reservation.'

For example: 'Some parents think it is very important to teach a child not to fight with other children, whereas other parents think that a child has to learn how to defend itself under special circumstances. What do you think?'

Balance every alternative with another which also contains a positive value judgement:

'Do you and your family think it is important to express your affection for each other openly or do you belong to the more reserved type of people . . .'

Use mild expressions. For example during an interview on education, expressions such as 'methods of education' or 'disciplinary methods' are preferable to 'methods of punishment'.

If the theme of the discussion involves criticism of another person or an institution, give the person questioned the opportunity to first express praise so that he won't feel he is being unfair.

For example:

'What do you like most about your foreman?'

followed by: 'What do you dislike the most?'

Introduce questions with words and phrases that don't undermine the other's self-worth:

'Do you happen to know the politician in your constituency?'

rather than 'Do you know . . .'

Pay attention to the formulation of indirect questions.

For example:

1. Make assumptions about the questionee and his behaviour that shift the weight of denial onto him. Kinsey (1948) used this technique when formulating his questions: 'When did you . . . for the first time?' rather than 'Did you ever?'[1]

2. Think about delicate questions you need to ask, and which requirements you want to consider and implicitly regard as fact. These indirect questions are usually opening questions initiating a new part of a dialogue and thus require careful preparation.

For example, a customer would like one agent to work as sub-contractor for a larger company. The central agency is opposed on the grounds that they want to take over all the areas and the sub-contractor because he sees no possibility for constructive co-operation.

Sub-contractor to customer: 'How can we counter these moves by the central agency to put our services to you in a bad light?'

REFERENCE

1. König, R.: 'Das Interview', 1965, P. 48.

6

THE FUNCTION OF QUESTIONS AND THE USE OF QUESTIONING TECHNIQUES

Questions have a specific function in the course of a dialogue or in its planning, such as introducing a topic, confirming opinions or drawing conclusions. We use questions in the same way that an iron bar can be used, to push, to twist, to pull, to lift, to lever, to wrench or to strike.

The selection of the appropriate question-type, its formulation and choice of words varies according to the function of the question and, of course, according to the conversation partner and the questioning situation.

1. OPENING QUESTIONS

Opening questions are broad questions that seek to elicit the conversation partner's opinions of his problems or interests; they relax the mood or atmosphere; often they deal with current topics of the day. These questions should give the partner the opportunity to introduce his position into the conversation. Often they contain assumptions which are accepted if the question elicits a response.

For example: 'What do you think of the current economic situation?'

'How do you see the situation in your department?'
'What do you think is the reason for the situation in your department?'

2. PERSONAL QUESTIONS

Personal questions are also called *motivating* questions and are very useful for opening a dialogue. This question-type includes all those questions which allow the partner to demonstrate his skills, knowledge, achievements, social position or other qualities of which he is proud. They have a positive influence on the climate of the conversation and are aimed at the self-image of the partner.
For example: 'What time did you make on the race circuit?'
'How did you fill that order?'
'How are the children?'
'Don't you have customers who put their highest demands on a product and are willing to put up with a high price because of its prestige value?'

3. CONCLUDING OR CONTINUATION QUESTIONS

This question-type is clearly the most effective. It quickly reaches its goal and is very useful. The partner must find the answer for himself because he then accepts it.
For example: 'If you had to travel by horse nowadays, would you prefer a thoroughbred or a draught horse?' (in response to the observation that high-horsepowered cars are no longer necessary for travel).
'What do you conclude from the low selection of stock and fast turnover?'
'What effect do exclusive products and a high standard of quality have on your sales?'

4. SPECIFIC INFORMATION QUESTIONS

These questions suggest reasons, motives and intentions that we need for our argumentation.

For example: 'How many people do you usually go on vacation with?'

'How do you view the learning motivation of your co-workers?'

'What potential do you see in this strategy?'

A particular type of specific information question is the *filter* question, which should define if the partner is at all capable of providing the desired information.

For example: 'Did you go to the last International Automobile Exhibition?'

'Do you know anything about the new orders?'

5. FOLLOW-UP QUESTIONS

These questions serve to elicit deeper and more detailed information to improve the questioner's understanding, to make the partner aware of what he expresses, and to make him commit himself to specific statements. By means of these questions the questioner can gain time, present his own arguments and learn about the opinions, experiences and prejudices of his conversation partner.

These questions are sometimes called *boomerang* questions because responses can be directed back to the questioner.

For example: 'How did you mean what you said just now?'

'What did you mean by . . . , for example?'

'In what way was the quality unsatisfactory?'

'Where do *you* see the disadvantage?'

'How did you come to such a point of view?'

6. QUESTIONS RELATING TO PROCEDURE (AGENDA)

On the one hand, these questions are impulses which, for the sake of form, are phrased as questions.
For example: 'How shall we proceed?'
'Do you agree that we put the main point first?'
On the other hand, these questions act as neutralizers when excitement runs high.
For example: 'Now if . . . , what would you do then?'
'Is it a hopeless case?'

7. ENCOURAGEMENTS

Stimulus is given by making remarks that are emotionally loaded and supportive of the conversation partner. This can be done through a change of tone that expresses surprise or contradiction, or by exaggeration.
For example: 'And what about security?'
'Do you mean you're going to resign?'
'Who doesn't want success?'
'There are always these environmental problems, aren't there?'
'Reliability is always a problem, isn't it?'

8. CHECKING QUESTIONS

In a sales interview these questions serve to bring about agreement and finalisation of essential issues; in a teaching conversation or an examination oral to find out the degree of knowledge of the student; in employee interviews and criminal interrogations to bring out contradictions or provide indications of honesty; for the consultant to assess his understanding of the consulting process. These different applications will be looked at in more detail in specific chapters.

7

PERSONNEL INTERVIEWS

Better contact and understanding through questions.

The development of a conversation and with it the willingness of the partner to respond and, therefore, the questioning technique used depend upon the numerous purposes of the personnel interview, such as:

1. the employment interview to select personnel;
2. the evaluation interview in cases of promotion or other personnel changes within the company;
3. the employee interview — a routine talk about opinions, points of view, the relationship of the worker to his job, his company and everything connected with it;
4. the counseling dialogue in which the worker is advised on his personal or professional problems;
5. the stress interview, with the purpose of testing the performance of the interviewee under a number of difficult conditions;
6. the feedback dialogue for information and motivation of workers through correction and approval;
7. the dismissal conversation, either to fire a worker or to discover the reasons for his resignation;
8. the task conversation, ranging from specific instructions to problem-solving meetings.

Here we would like to explore the employment interview and the critical review conversation as examples of a relevant questioning technique. A separate chapter has been devoted to the counseling dialogue because of its wider range of application.

THE EMPLOYMENT INTERVIEW

'The right man in the right place.'

'Anything goes' is the most common motto of all employment interviews. Tricks, bluffing, tactical manoeuvers and much caution are among the factors that influence the conversation situation. The applicant is overly motivated and tries to rationalize everything; the interviewer counters with the cool calculation of a specialist judging a salesman who tries to sell himself. In spite of the hard sell, the applicant must appear genuine and honest (at least) in order to succeed.

The interviewer is under an obligation to find the best man for a particular job. He cannot fall for a bluff nor, on the other hand, can he afford to send the best man away. Often the situation is quite tense because of the differing wavelengths of the two conversation partners. The complications that this can create have already been outlined in Chapter 2 in the notes on 'the first impression'. Ideally, a first impression should give *the* total image of the conversation partner, but this may be asking too much from even the best psychologist. It is therefore a good idea to limit oneself with respect to content before developing the conversation.

— Keep the conversation simple by using a written questionnaire for neutral (non-critical) information.
— Restrict yourself to:
a) themes that are usually presented in a 'positive' light, such as reasons for resignation, hobbies, personal problems, likes and

Reception
— a friendly reception of the applicant from the moment he walks in the door will determine his first impression;
— applicant is led to prepared reception room immediately and told who will participate in the interview. Positions of people receiving to be made clear;
— no telephone activity in the reception room, no interruptions;
— applicant should not have to wait long but his papers should be carefully checked before reception;
— the interview should have an objective character and should not hide the negative aspects of the position under discussion;
— the behaviour of the applicant is often influenced by insecurity and nervousness; therefore, avoid an interrogation style, loosen up and create an atmosphere that is friendly, straightforward and inspires confidence.

Opening of talk
— friendly reception;
— thanks for the visit;
— enquiries about journey, accommodation (if applicable);
— enquire about cost of journey and other expenses with a view to reimbursement by the administration;
— refer to *curriculum vitae* which has been studied prior to interview, questions about points that are unclear or gaps in time sequence;
— questions about reasons for considered change of employment, whether applicant has already given notice, whether possible to question present employer;
— if necessary, questions about degrees, references;
— questioning about applicant's expectations, how does he view his prospective job, etc.

Orientation of the applicant
(provided impression remains positive)
— his future sphere of activity, description of his function and
  his position in the hierarchy, responsibilities, working relationship to other departments, composition of personnel in
  his department;
— initial working-in and probability of promotion and ad-
  vancement (e.g. management training), salary or pay scale,
  possibilities for further training within the company, (possible reimbursement for moving house, etc).

Questioning the applicant
— how far does the post described meet his expectations? why
  does he think he is qualified for it? does he feel there are weak
  points? does he have any special wishes? (according to interview plan);
— further questions about change of address, agreement of marriage partner, starting date, possible handicaps, personal rec-
  ord, personal problems (financial worries, intended divorce,
  serious past illnesses and their effects), expected salary, long-
  term or short-term position.

Practical questions
— discussion of conditions of employment (to extent that applicant is still interested in the post);
— discussion of employment contract (if standardized), otherwise discussion including the following points:
  • starting date
  • working hours per week, per day (breaks)
  • annual leave (and additional requirements relating to
    length of service)
  • leave under special circumstances (marriage, death within
    family or of friends, births, military service, moving house)

- public duties (committee member, expert, etc.) and time needed annually
- payment of salary, extra pay or bonus, 13-month payment, profit sharing, car and travel expenses, free board and lodging, pension fund/company insurance
- type of accident insurance, interest rate for pension fund, savings insurance, company medical insurance
- working-in procedure
- possibilities of training within the company or mandatory training
- probation period
- termination clause
- possible competition clause.

Remaining points
— clear statement of agreement that has been reached (how binding or not), when to report back;
— if another applicant is chosen, immediate notification will be given;
— giving a company brochure (value in family discussion as well as in the general sense of advertising).

Evaluation of the interview
Write down immediately all important details and impressions, especially with a view to later comparison with other applicants.

Plan for an employment interview

Professional
1. In your previous profession, what were your main tasks?
   Why did you put them in that order?
   How much time did you need approximately for each one of

these tasks?

Did you find this definition of your task area meaningful?

Which tasks do you think should have been delegated to other people?

Which task did you find the most interesting and personally satisfying?

How did the post become vacant?

Why do you think you were chosen for the job?

2. What training do you consider a necessary requirement for your present position?

3. What special problems arise in your present job?

Do you think such problems are typical of your job or concern the company as a whole?

Which problems concern you most?

How do you approach these problems?

How would you describe your present superior?

How would you describe your concept of leadership?

4. How has your job changed since you occupied the position?

What part did you play in that change?

5. What evidence of your work do you see remaining in that company?

How did you achieve that?

Were these results planned or did they simply follow from your work?

6. How would you describe your development in that company?

How would you compare it with that of others who joined the company at the same time?

Would you have made a different choice if more information had been available to you?

7. How does your present job compare with your previous position? Which do you prefer?

What difficulties of adjustment or other problems arose with the change?
8. How would you justify your employment to a potential employer?

Personal
1. From your professional experience taken as a whole, what specific qualities do you see in yourself?
2. In what area(s) of your profession do you feel not especially competent?
3. What characteristics and aptitudes do you personally consider good?
4. Everyone has faults and weaknesses. What are yours?
5. What is your professional goal in the medium- or long-term?
6. How does the position under discussion help you to achieve this goal?
7. What was it that interested you about our advertisement? What attracts you to this post?
8. Looking back over your life, what do you regard as exceptional successes?
9. What mistakes would you not repeat?
10. Does your professional life influence your family life?
11. How would you describe the education of your parents?
12. Do you know of any other information relevant to the evaluation of your application?

CRITICAL REVIEW CONVERSATION
Questions — insight — behaviour change

Questions are a means to an end and with the critical review conversation we can try to put right things that have gone wrong. Criticism is one type of feedback used by the boss, for example, when a worker has deliberately shown (due to lack of motivation) negative behaviour (wastage, absenteeism) or makes repeated mistakes.

A minor error caused by hurrying or forgetfulness is corrected by a specific order (quasi-instructions): 'What did we say was the exact tolerance?' or 'Could you also check that item 5 on the form is always filled in because it determines who is responsible?'

To create willingness to accept criticism, which takes the form of listening and answering constructively, there is one condition to be met. A rule of thumb: the ratio of positive feedback (confirmation, approval) to negative feedback (correction, criticism) should be not less than 2:1. This ratio is achieved easily if numerous checks are made and good performance is met with 'OK', 'In order' and 'Correct'. Often excessive tension enters the critical review conversation because the boss thinks he can overreact. In his anger over a mistake, he wants to let off steam. At this point three deep breaths in ten seconds can be helpful! The critical review conversation should take place before the mistake occurs again. The guy who thinks he's perfect and knows everything can immediately start criticizing whereas normal people have to find out what happened and why! The first part of a critical review conversation is therefore not an accusation but an information question. If dealing with a factual problem, discussion shouldn't take place before an audience as one of the conversation partners will always try to avoid losing face.

Correct development of a critical review conversation (with the most probable question-types) looks something like this:
0. preparation, gathering factual information;
1. choosing a favourable time, like after the break;
2. creating a positive, normal atmosphere, — not too long, one or two opening questions;
3. statement of the problem in a quiet, objective manner including your own information without guesswork;

4. asking the viewpoint of the conversation partners (information questions);
5. giving insight into the consequences for workers and boss (possibly concluding questions), agreement on evaluation of problem (suggestive-confirmation questions);
6. discovering reasons for negative behaviour (within reason; open questions first, possibly followed by closed and suggestive questions);
7. determining future course of action and future behaviour of all conversation partners (with the participation of those being criticized), elimination of probable causes (concluding open-information questions, possibly suggestive-confirmation questions);
8. clear statement of further action, obtaining the approval of all criticized (suggestive-confirmation questions);
9. set up a check system, determine what type of checks (open and alternative-suggestive questions);
10. create positive close of conversation.

From the above, what other conclusions can we draw about questioning technique? In the information stage, the more the boss speaks, the less he will get to know. If he uses questions aimed at checking his guesses, he will not discover anything new when his guesses are wrong. At the beginning only one method works and that is using broad and open questions. The co-worker can then describe clearly what happened or the version the boss should hear. Besides, several consecutive closed questions give the impression of an interrogation, which should not be the case in a critical review conversation.

While listening to the worker's description, you can check it for credibility. The more the other speaks, the quicker he will be caught up in contradictions. In the critical review conversation the choice of words plays an important role because the words used are interpreted in terms of the relationship between the partners. *For example:*

transmitter says	*receiver interprets*
— better	— worse
— faster	— lame duck
— more efficient	— fusspot
— more thorough	— sloppy
— more economical	— spendthrift

Occasionally you face the problem of it being preferable not to discover everything because you would then be obliged to act strictly according to the rules and against your better judgement. In this case, use a *cover* question but make sure that the hidden question is equally understood on both sides. This will depend on the similar wavelengths or the degree of familiarity the partners have developed through past cooperation. Thus, when a head of a research department asks his engineer or designer, 'Where did you find the solution?', he possibly wants to express his criticism or disapproval of copying a competitor. If the engineer fails to perceive the criticism, he will proudly proceed to show the difficulties he has had to overcome in order to arrive at the final draft.

Suppose you discover that your employees are taking days off to work on the side. You don't want to dismiss them because they are good workers but you have to put an end to their negative behaviour. In this case, you could be working with insinuations or talking in generalizations:

'You're a good bricklayer too, aren't you?'

(Suggestive questions allow only a yes/no answer.)

'Why do you work on construction sites at the weekend?'

(Indirect questioning also asking for reasons for negative behaviour.)

'At the same time, you are often absent.'

(Clear, objective statement.)

'How do you think the company is affected by absenteeism?'

(Open-information question dealing with the problem of his absence without wanting to know more reasons for it.)

'You need to earn more money. Would you be interested in doing some overtime or extra work on Saturdays here, which might save you from, hmm . . . getting sick on a windy construction site?'

(Observation followed by an alternative question where the tone is suggestive and the choice of words — 'hmm . . . getting sick' — is ambiguous.)

This example shows clearly that questioning technique depends on the purpose of the question and the questioning situation; the answer depends on the partner's opinion of the questioner.

So much for the theory. Here is a practical example of a critical review conversation.

Conversation partner: Mrs. Shellman, clerk, 28 years. She has been employed for ten years and occupies a clerical position in the administration of a magazine. She is married and occasionally hints at marital problems. She is known to be very reliable and orderly. At 5 p.m. her job, which she is not especially interested in, is over. She is neither overworked nor underworked. Her relationship with her boss and her colleagues is normal. Her boss never shouts but is very demanding. Criticism has rarely been necessary in the past. Flexible working hours.

Problem: She suddenly shows negligence in the last two weeks with her filing and has been told about it twice already.

Purpose: To discover the reasons and to ensure more careful filing in the future.

Willingness to answer varies with each question.

After the lunch break.

Boss: 'Good afternoon, Mrs. Shellman. Please sit down. It's nice to have a walk during the lunch break when the weather is so pleasant, isn't it?'

She: 'Yes, it's just a pity that it doesn't last longer.'

Boss: 'Would you prefer to have a longer lunch break and go home later?'

She: 'For heaven's sake, no. I prefer the shorter break.'

Boss: 'You say that with such emphasis.'

She: 'Ah, well, at least to get home before my husband.'

Boss: 'Is that so important?'

She: 'Yes.'

Boss: 'Well, Mrs. Shellman, I wanted to speak to you about your filing. These last few days I couldn't find some papers and while looking for them I came across a letter from Miller filed with Meadows. I didn't understand and so I wanted to talk to you about it.'

She: 'Oh, it must have got there by mistake.'

Boss: 'And what about the others I was looking for?'

She: 'They are filed. I don't understand that.'

Boss: 'Neither do I. Your written work, everything else is well done. Up until now, so was the filing. Now suddenly in the last eight to ten days . . .? Do you have some problems I don't know about?'

She: 'Up until now, I had more time for filing. But these days I have to finish all the correspondence by half past four and the filing must be done everyday in the late afternoon.'

Boss: 'But don't you have enough time for that? Could you come later in the morning?'

She: 'But I have to be home when my husband arrives.'

Boss: 'Right. You have to be home by 5.30 p.m. Let's look at it from the company's point of view. Why do you think it's so important

8
THE
TEACHING CONVERSATION

Teaching through questions.

'It's up to you whether you think it's useful to ask the student questions he can't answer to make him realize that there is still a lot to be learned.'

If you ask someone what he understands by 'teaching', the kind of answers you receive will be: to transmit information, to pass on knowledge, to communicate experience. These concepts suggest the lecture as a teaching method. Only when you ask about the purpose of teaching activity does it become clearer that its objective is the learning process of the participants, i.e. the activity of the teacher should consist primarily in creating the optimal conditions for this process to take place.

Of course, a certain content must be learned and where it is factual, lectures with notes, films, slides and books are efficient ways of providing information.

In relation to understanding and learning concepts, rules and strategies of problem-solving, i.e. when thinking is involved, stimulus through an active teaching method is surely the better choice. The best known active teaching method is the teaching conversation which develops through questioning.

What advantages do questions offer? Above all, questions create activity and we now know that learning success is somewhat proportional to activity. The more active we are, the more likely we are to benefit. These questions also allow the teacher to check on understanding and see what is retained. He can adjust himself to the learning level and speed of his students, correcting mistakes where necessary and, more importantly, confirming correct answers. The student experiences confirmation as success; the more successful we are in a situation, the better we feel and the more we want to continue learning.

FORMULATION

Especially important: Fix short-term learning goals and write them on a blackboard with key words. You then have a goal and the content. If you act in accordance with teaching principles (tried and tested after all), going from the known (to the learner) to the unknown, you first work out the theory and then add specific details. In this way, your framework is already established.

If I had to teach the following short-term learning goals:
1. define the concept of the 'balance sheet';
2. determine which parts of the balance sheet are passive and which are active;
3. evaluate the financial stability of a modern business;
then I would start with 2. because all students are surely familiar with parts of it. Then 1. and finally 3.

Now let's go on to the strategy of formulating questions:
— decide which answer (from the blackboard) you want to hear first;
— think about one or more questions which most of your students should be able to answer (see Chapter 5 on individual criteria for formulation);
— one of the most promising methods is to draw on examples and comparisons from everyday life or from the student's experience. Through the comparison, the idea 'clicks' and the student tries to apply the principle of the comparison to the new question (see examples at end of chapter);

— consider whether it is possible to answer your question differently, given the particular background of experience and expectations of the students;
— sharpen your question so that irrelevant answers will be excluded. If this is not possible, devise a question that leads the conversation back to the learning pathway.

The teacher who likes to hear himself speak will formulate a question like the following:

'If we think about the interests of a worker, now or in the future, especially in the current economic situation, in his relationship with his boss and colleagues, certain motives become apparent. Therefore, I would now like to ask you what reasons could lead the worker to react to the given situation in this way rather than in any other?'

Such long-winded formulations indicate that the teacher is either verbose, lacking in concentration or just isn't taking his students into account. Surely the student will be able to answer more easily if the question were formulated thus: 'Why does a worker act in this way?'

You won't like this question either: 'How do you classify societies?' 'What societies?' you ask, and rightly so because there is more than one way of classifying societies, e.g., sociologically (communist, liberal, capitalist) and economically (corporation, partnership, guild). The question is not clear.

The question, 'What makes brakes work?' is also not clear as we don't know whether it is the principle or the mechanism that is being questioned.

Here are two questions, supposedly asking the same thing:

'What attitudes would preoccupy your awareness given a condition of thirst motivation as you proceeded along the thoroughfares of an urban environment?'
'What do you notice first walking through city streets when you are thirsty?'

Why make a simple question so complicated? The student finds it more difficult — at least it takes him longer to understand. And the teacher needs an answer, rather than to teach the student how to understand questions of varying degrees of complexity! It is the content that is important to him.

Certain grammatical forms also make it easier for the student to understand the question. When the sentence addressed to him starts with a verb or a question word he feels immediately that he is being spoken to and is motivated to answer. The inverted question is grammatically incorrect and may be perceived as a surprise attack. The student may be inattentive, miss part of a question and suddenly be confronted with the part he didn't hear.

'If we call the teaching conversation a method which develops through questioning, then the central point is what?'

'If we call the teaching conversation a method which develops through questioning, then what is its central point?'

Questions which are grammatically incorrect indicate that the questioner originally intended to make a statement but, remembering a little too late his purpose of making the students think, tries to turn his statement into a question — clear proof of insufficient preparation.

As the teaching conversation and its content have to develop simultaneously, the questions should be built onto each other, which means that the next question has to take into account the answer of the question preceding it.

Question: 'What advantages does the teaching conversation offer in contrast to the lecture method?'
Answer: 'Greater activity, adjustment to the student, corrections, confirmation as a source of motivation.'
Question: 'How is this activity created?'
Answer: 'Through questioning.'

Question: 'What is therefore the most important factor for the teacher in this method?'
Answer: 'The mastery of questioning dialogue.'

If the grapes hang too high, i.e. if the questions are too difficult, the student is not motivated to even try to think. The level of complexity of the question should take into account intelligence, knowledge and practice in answering questions as well as willingness to reply. Whether or not a question is adequate can only be known after we receive an answer. The teacher comes to know his group quite quickly and judges from experience which questions can be categorized as difficult or easy. Questions like:

'How long did the Thirty Years' War last?'

'Who manufactured the model-T Ford?'

are obviously inadequate because they are too simple. Questions asked in this way are generally regarded as boring and childish. We should always consider the teaching conversation as a way of guiding the thought process of the student in a given direction and unnecessary detours should be avoided. A distinction should be made between goal-directed questions, which are relevant, and superfluous questions which can be omitted. Questions which are too general in scope lead away from the goal, leaving the way open for distractions. For example:

'What do you think of the office of Prime Minister?'
'What is an instructor supposed to do?'

Conversely, questions which are too narrow in scope leave little space for creative thought. This type of question is found in programmed learning:

'What are the three main parts of an essay?'
Int- - - - -, Dev- - - - -, Con- - - - -

In principle, every teaching conversation is different because the questions used are not standardized. As the teaching situation always varies, one has to improvise continually when formulating questions. When we realize from the answer we receive that our question was inadequate, we replace it with a more precise question. Such an accumulation of questions may be confusing for the student. Neither will asking obvious questions ('How many sides has a triangle?') nor simply checking knowledge stimulate thought. These so-called low-order questions are only permissible as checking questions, usually placed at the beginning of a teaching conversation to assess existing knowledge or at the end to determine what has been understood and absorbed. High-order questions require consequential or deductive thinking:

'Why does the sun rise in the east?'
'How can you solve this problem?'
'What are your reasons for choosing this method?'

The teacher wanting to guide the thinking of his students into set patterns will ask stereotyped questions or questions with the same beginning and the same goal. In contrast, unexpected questions not only brighten the atmosphere but also develop the critical faculties of the student in relation to what he is being taught, leading of course to uncomfortable, i.e. critical, questions from the student to the teacher.

HOW TO ASK A QUESTION

'Miller, can you give me an example of reciprocity in cultural behaviour?'

Miller turns from white to red, looks around the room and after a few seconds he starts stuttering. With this question, and by first calling out his name, we've really done it! We've managed to create a thinking block in the student and to make him feel like a failure. Moreover, the others in the class have all relaxed on the assumption that Miller is handling the question. Thus the meaning of the question has been distorted in both directions. A question should therefore be addressed to everyone and followed by a pause (because thinking takes time); someone is then called upon to answer (necessary in training groups) or the question is taken up by a volunteer (e.g. in adult education courses). Nervous, drawn-out speech is as bad as that which is not loud enough, mumbled or otherwise unclear. If the questioner shows how 'interested' he is in an answer through the indifferent and condescending tone of his question, he will be overwhelmed with similar 'interest' from his students! Quiet intonation, encouragement and normal speech stimulate conversation flow and thus motivation to participate in the thinking activity. It is a bad habit to encourage rapid responses as then the lazy stay lazy. In new groups, it is advisable to give time and attention to volunteers initially; later on it is more worthwhile to include the quiet ones and restrain the over-enthusiastic.

Because some students cannot think quickly enough, in some cases it may be better to answer the questions oneself! Another stimulus consists of repeating frequently one's own questions or the answers that were given! As a precaution against over-involvement in the learning activity, it may be preferable to ask questions to which only 'yes' or 'no' can be the answer. For example, 'Did you understand?' or 'Is this a square or a trapezium?'

Invaluable of course are those suggestive questions that discourage unnecessary critical attitudes or objectionable creativity!

Anyway, students are not especially articulate and it might be better to ask them only words or to complete parts of sentences!

For example: 'A sentence consists of a subject and a predi_____.'

An effective way of avoiding trust in the relationship is the question trap. Wait until the student is not on the ball and then ask an extremely difficult or misleading question. It is very likely he won't be able to answer or, if he does, he will get it wrong. You can then put the student in his place! If you use this tactic several times, you may be sure you won't be bothered by over-enthusiastic students during breaks.

If you have interpreted these suggestions as warnings rather than as recommendations, you are on the right track.

THE FUNCTION OF THE QUESTION
IN TEACHING CONVERSATIONS

To avoid being disloyal to our definition of the teaching conversation as a method which develops through generating questions, we begin with the most important question-type, which is the *basic theme* or *working question*. Students are encouraged to observe, think and, if possible, find answers to this for themselves. Following which you may often have to ask *complementary questions* ('What else?' and 'Besides that?') or *questions concerning reasons* ('Why?', 'What for?', 'How did you come to that conclusion?'). When you ask a question about a decision related to a specific situation (e.g. 'Can the computer now work with the other data?' or 'Which of these possibilities do you think is more valid?'), the question concerning the rationale for the answer cannot be avoided.

Another function of the question in the teaching conversation is checking on knowledge; this may be done at the beginning, during the course or at the end as assessment. Often a teacher asks his students: 'Have you understood?', and the reaction is no reaction as the students are uncertain about whether they really have understood. It is therefore more practical to use real checking questions that verify understanding by asking for factual information.

QUESTIONER FEEDBACK

'Well, if you take your time at the examination, I can guarantee you good results.'

'You should also think about your answer before you open your mouth.'

'Rubbish! Didn't you hear what I said?'

What effect do these different types of teacher-reaction have on the students? If you react in this way, you should count on a similar reaction from your students: they will either become aggressive or totally indifferent. If correct answers are acknowledged and confirmed they are memorized much more easily, whereas if you fail to correct mistakes, it is the mistakes that are memorized.

The first type of questioner feedback is therefore related to content (*positive verbal reinforcement,* see checklist.)

The second type of questioner feedback is *positive non-verbal reinforcement,* which enriches the context or mood in which the question is asked, showing interest in the answer or in the student through nodding of the head etc.

However, if the answers given are incomplete or incorrect, we employ a third type of questioner feedback known as *positive limited reinforcement.* An insufficient answer can be indicated by means of *connecting* questions, repeating the question in a modified form ('Think about it for a moment . . .') or passing the question onto the group ('Does everyone agree with that?'). Never treat an answer condescendingly, for example, 'I didn't

CHECKLIST: QUESTIONING TECHNIQUE IN TEACHING CONVERSATION

⊕   ⊖

1. Formulation

⊕	⊖
— short	— long-winded
— precise	— complicated
— clear	— misleading
— simple	— complex
— grammatically correct	— grammatically incorrect
— beginning with a verb or question word	— inverted
— logical	— illogical
— adequate (answerable)	— too easy/difficult
— goal-directed (relevant)	— superfluous (irrelevant)
— limiting	
— no accumulation	— two or more questions
— high-order questions	— obvious questions
— unusual questions	— stereotyped questions
— question impulses	

2. How to ask a question

⊕	⊖
— question everyone	— name in front of question
— a pause after the question	— no thinking time given
— audible and clear	— low and unclear
— quiet tones	— nervous, drawn out
— encouraging	— indifferent, condescending
— calling on individuals	
— volunteers	

3. Mistakes

— repeating your own question
— answering your own question yourself
— repeating answers
— questions with yes/no answers
— suggestive questions
— questions with syllables as answers
— question traps

CHECKLIST: QUESTIONER FEEDBACK

1. *Positive Verbal Reinforcement*
   — react to student's expression of feeling
   — express understanding
   — react to content of student's contribution
   — simple feedback ('Yes', 'Right', nodding head)
   — precise feedback: give requirements and compare with work
   — encouragement for further work
   — express personal opinion ('I think . . .')
   — acknowledge student's progress
   — modify student's contribution (make it more precise)
   — emphasize importance of student's contribution

2. *Positive Non-verbal Reinforcement*
   — active listening
   — showing your optimism
   — looking for contact, positive behaviour, paying attention
   — relating to group

3. *Positive Limited Reinforcement*
   — ask for explanation of learning pathway
   — put contribution up for discussion
   — acknowledge student's effort
   — clear up points still unclear

4. *Positive Subsequent Reinforcement*
   — employ student's expressions
   — incorporate student's contribution for future development

5. *Positive Reinforcement of Learning Atmosphere*
   — remaining silent
   — eye contact
   — giving guidance
   — helpful, constructive behaviour
   — giving a feeling of involvement

Mistakes

— close physical contact
— indifference
— reacting unenthusiastically or with hostility to questions
— offending, ironic or disrespectful answers

— ignoring questions
— referring to student as stupid
— making fun of student's expressions
— failing to correct mistakes

mean the question that way', 'I'm looking for a different answer . . .', or 'You're already way ahead of me'. If the thinking was logical, acknowledge the answer and ask a new question.

Positive questioner feedback can also be created through using the contributions or responses of the students for future work (*fourth positive reinforcement*).

The fifth aspect of positive behaviour relates to creating a positive learning atmosphere. The questions of the teacher, lecturer or instructor are basically checking questions, in that the questioner generally knows the answers already. The teacher wants the student to find the answer for himself and to show to what extent he has successfully mastered the content; in other words that he can answer the question adequately.

PRACTICE EXAMPLE OF QUESTIONING TECHNIQUE FOR TEACHING
(Please analyse using the table on page 112.)

We don't live like hermits but in groups such as the family, the office, the classroom or the club. We all have to *communicate* through words, gestures, writing and images. Especially when you are leader of a study group, this becomes a necessity. It is therefore important to ensure that the people we communicate with *receive* and understand our *information*. Let's look a little more closely at information-receiving, after which you should be able to list the main factors that influence *perception*.

1. Which types of perception do you know?
   ──────────► seeing, hearing, touching, tasting, smelling, telepathy

2. What does our perception depend upon?

PERCEPTION
seeing, hearing, tasting, smelling, feeling

SELECTION

OBJECT	ENVIRONMENT	SUBJECT
(perceived)		(perceiver)
order	background	ability to perceive
contrast	frame of reference	motivation
quantity	structure	expectations
		experience

OBJECT (perceived)

3. In which diagram do you recognize the number of dots more quickly and easily?

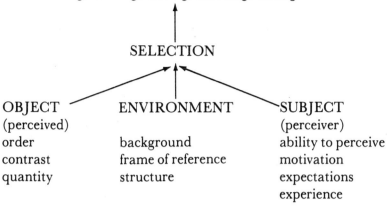

———→ in the one that is ordered (structure)

4. If you go for a walk at night down town, in what way do the night clubs attract your attention?

    ———→ with light

    Why does the light attract your attention?

    ———→ contrast

5. Surely you have noticed in car advertisements that not all advantages are listed. Why is that?

    ———→ quantity, not too much information at once

ENVIRONMENT

6. What do you see here?

━━━━━━▶ a vase, two profiles

7. What is the factor that determines whether you see a vase or
   two profiles?

   ━━━━━━▶ the choice between background and foreground

8. You have probably seen photographs of military manoeuvers where all the tanks and vehicles are painted and cov-
   ered with bushes. Why is that?

   ━━━━━━▶ for *camouflage*

9. What is it that enables camouflage to be effective?

   ━━━━━━▶ there is no distinction between background and
           foreground. Uniform *structure,* no contrast.

10. Apart from the environment and the object perceived, what
    is perception dependent upon?

    ━━━━━━▶ on the PERCEIVER

From recent studies, we know that:
3.10^6 bits meet the eye every second
2.10^4 bits meet the ear every second
A bit is a unit used for measuring information as a mile is a
unit of distance (e.g. the two words 'the house' consist of 15
bits). We are not able to process all the information we are
exposed to.

11. What results from this?
          → *selection*
12. What determines what a person sees?
          → his ability to see
13. What determines what he perceives?
          → his psychological make-up
14. If you walk for two hours through dusty streets in the heat, what do you notice?
          → drinks, advertisements, bars
15. Why?
          → *motivation*
16. It has often been found that teachers overlook the mistakes of their good students. Why?
          → positive *expectations*
17. Sometimes a driver will reach for the handbrake if there is a smell in the car. Why?
          → handbrake may be on
18. Why does he react specifically to the handbrake?
          → past *experience*

CHECK

19. What three factors determine how much and what we perceive?
          → environment, object (perceived) and subject (perceiver)
20. Why is the quantity of information important to perception?
          → too much cannot be absorbed
21. What factors cause selection of given information in an individual?
          → ability to perceive, motivation, expectations and experience.

9

THE ORAL EXAMINATION

Crucial decisions through questioning technique.

'Without a doubt the deciding factor for the success of an examination is the guiding and planning of the oral'

(Döring)

Often a bad examination is a badly prepared examination since a candidate's performance depends as much upon the preparation of the examiner as on his own. If you consider the likely consequences of an examination on a candidate's career, a careful preparation of content and questioning technique is the least an examiner can do to fulfill his obligations. It is limited to consider only the candidate's role in an examination situation, which is really much more complex.

'Examinations are situations in which an individual is given an opportunity to prove to a person or committee who have the right to examine that he possesses special qualifications, i.e. knowledge, skills, aptitudes, etc. The candidate offers this proof to enter effectively fields of learning or activity without harming those who have confidence in the qualifications.' (Flechsig)

The examiner creates the examination situation through his perception of his role and what he sees as the purpose of an examination. In our opinion, the purpose of an examination is to stimulate a candidate's ability through optimal use of questions which provide a basis of evaluation. Others see the purpose of exams as being to evaluate exactly what has been learned so as to predict under examination stress the future performance of a candidate in his profession. These two differing points of view about an examination's purpose result in two opposite modes of examining, namely 'from above' or 'from below'. The examiner 'from above' aims at locating weaknesses in his candidate and inferring what he has learned from what remains. He therefore begins with the most difficult questions and slowly works down the scale (consecutive order of failure).

The examiner determines whether examination goals are reached, that is whether relevant subject material is present. This can be a systematic process (tutorial) or a random process as with the quiz-master who asks questions from this and the other subject to cover in total the examination's scope. In the opinion of psychologists, it is reaction time, stress tolerance and cunning that is measured by this method rather than a candidate's competence. If, in spite of this, you still prefer examining 'from above', it is preferable to ask numerous, specific questions that are representative of the overall aim.

In an examination 'from below', the examiner starts with a very low level of difficulty because he sees his role as *conversation partner or helper* with candidates having particular psychological problems. A candidate should have the opportunity of using his ability as much as he can. Therefore, even the most difficult questions should stimulate discussion of different points of view. With an exam 'from below' you should give more thought and verbal stimuli and your questions should be wider in scope. Avoid checking questions, encourage activity and reinforce positive responses. Be willing to listen.

No matter which examination situation you prefer, all questions should be precise, clear, to the point and as short as possible. An accumulation of questions or an inverted question which does not begin with a verb or questioning word should be avoided. Suggestions in a false direction (question traps) are unethical and suggestions in a desired direction (leading questions) are likewise not in keeping with the examination's purpose. If necessary, you should paraphrase a question or concept misunderstood by the candidate before asking him to answer. Thus at the point of asking the question, a distinction can already be made between what is relevant and what is superfluous, and the requirement of a well-formulated question is met.

In all cases, lack of clarity in the content and in the type of response required should be avoided. In this respect, clear, obvious and ample explanations are helpful.

Generally, the following questioning is employed:

1. Examination questions asked spontaneously by the examiner (open questions, who-, what-, why-, how-questions and problem questions);
2. Preformulated questions and problem questions from reference files;
3. Questions dealing with subject areas chosen by the candidate in accordance with his inclination and specialization. Preformulated questions are standardized but do not take into account individual differences between candidates.

DEVELOPING THE EXAMINATION CONVERSATION

1. The examiner defines the scope of the examination and outlines its frame of reference. It has been shown that psychologically this enables a candidate to understand and classify individual questions more effectively.
2. The examiner relaxes the atmosphere by asking an elementary question that even the most nervous candidate could answer. Distracting themes rarely reduce nervousness because a candidate is only waiting for the first shot to be fired and so tension is probably increased. The feedback from the first question then is that it is really not so bad and the first

positive reinforcement ('correct') eases this tension and creates a more conversational mood.

3. The examiner then continues with a theme suggested by the candidate, taking short notes on question goals and progressively raising the level of difficulty.

   Bloom classifies the following levels of difficulty in ascending order:
   — verification and reproducing of knowledge;
   — evaluation of understanding;
   — use of skills and their practical application;
   — analysis and structuring of problems;
   — critical evaluation of factual material.

4. If you receive feedback from a candidate's incorrect answers that he has reached his limit, avoid giving (out of misguided sympathy) further questions which could create a failure experience (resulting in nervousness and apprehension), and move into a new subject area.

5. Give immediate feedback to the candidate as to whether his answer is right or wrong; avoid implicit criticism, such as 'Didn't you learn anything at all?' or 'Don't you know that?'

Every examination situation should follow the structure of a teaching conversation, as the questioning technique used is similar. Therefore, refer to the teaching conversation as your example.

10

THE SALES CONVERSATION

Guiding sales talks through questioning.

'Most negotiators talk too much.' (Stangl)

Surely you have noticed that listening creates a friendly atmosphere whereas talking leads to defensiveness. Did you ever have a sales conversation where you described all the advantages of your product in the rosiest colours right down to the last detail and in the end the customer made a clumsy excuse to avoid buying your product?

On the other hand, you may have had many sales conversations where you responded to your customer, asked questions, let him talk, even encouraged him to talk, and when the time came for clinching the deal there was no resistance. Even without your saying everything you knew about the product, the customer bought it.

Like certain other types of conversation, a sales conversation passes through several stages. Depending upon the product to be sold, some stages will be dropped and others added. However, one always proceeds from finding out about the needs of the customer and defining his aims to the final contract, a process in which the customer is increasingly influenced and guided by the sales consultant. It is also possible to make a quick sale where the aim is not to develop a regular client but rather to manipulate the one-time customer. You have to decide which type of situation you are interested in. Your conversation tactic, and therefore your questioning technique, will depend upon this choice.

Your strategy will vary depending upon whether you want to sell known (trade-registered) products that cannot be easily modified, or services. There are many similarities but one shouldn't overlook the differences.

For example, services are sold by insurance representatives, craftsmen, beauticians, transport and travel agencies, cleaners, architects and other independent professionals, advertising agencies, technical development departments and educational institutes.

Let's take this example of strategy used for selling the services in a beauty salon. The following is taken from a tapescript of a dialogue between a hair-dresser (H) and a client (C) who is the wife of a police constable and has been a customer for one year. She has an appointment.

H: 'Good morning, Mrs. Summer. I'll be right with you. How are you? Would you mind taking a seat over there?'

C: 'I'm quite well, thank you. And tonight is the Policeman's Ball.'

H: 'Then of course you would like something special. Do you know already what you'd like?'

C: 'I'd like something that suits me, but I don't mind a surprise.'

H: 'Let's do something completely different then. And as you're going out, I suggest a complete facial and then when you go home you won't have to do anything except dress. From what I see, you have tiny spots on your skin which must irritate you a lot. Have you had them long?'

C: 'Yes, they do irritate me quite a bit. I've had them quite often over the last few weeks. I have a brand of make-up at home, but I must say I don't have confidence in it anymore.'

H: 'What do you mean? What do you use at home?'

C: 'I use a cleansing milk and a face lotion that burns a lot and then I have a day cream and a night cream.'

H: 'You said the face lotion burns a lot which means it may contain a lot of alcohol. Do you use it to remove the cleansing milk?'

C: 'No, I remove the cleansing milk with water. But what if the face lotion is high in alcohol? I'm no expert and as far as I know it's not written on the bottle.'

H: 'Well, I would really like to make a skin test for you. The lotion burns and you have small spots on your cheeks which is usually an indication that the skin needs something. It looks nicer if the skin under the make-up is healthy.'

C: 'Yes, of course. I would like to know what state my skin is in as I'm not quite sure about it.'

H: 'What do you think your skin needs at the moment?'

C: 'I don't know what it needs. I only know how it feels. Sometimes it's practically dripping. Here, the forehead and everywhere. Other times, it's completely dry. It's crazy.'

H: 'What effect does the dryness have? Does your skin peel?'

C: 'Yes, it does.'

H: 'Is it itchy as well?'

C: 'Yes.'

H: 'Does it feel tight?'

C: 'No, not really.'

H: 'Does it go red?'

C: 'Yes, and it's also sensitive when it's cold or when I'm nervous.'

H: 'You have a job as well, don't you? When you work a lot, does it seem to affect you more?'

C: 'Yes, and then there's the housework.'

H: 'You also have two children?'

C: 'Yes, and my husband changes his shifts. That's a strain, sometimes.'

H: 'Well, Mrs. Summer, I have just completed your skin test and I find that your skin is perfectly normal as far as its oil content is concerned but that it lacks moisture to a very high degree. This explains why it feels tight and itchy.'

C: 'But it isn't tight, it just itches.'

H: 'I forgot that. (Looks into card index system.) You said you use a moisturizing cream but your skin still badly lacks moisture. I'll make a short treatment to prepare your skin. This will moisten the surface of your skin and looks nice afterwards. The trouble is you can't make up for what has been neglected at home in one session here.'

C: 'I understand that very well.'

H: 'The red spots will disappear if you treat your skin morning and evening as you've been doing but with preparations that are suited to your particular skin type. Let me show you some of the preparations I would like to use for treating your skin. This is a cleansing milk for deep-cleansing your skin. It is important because it makes your skin more absorbent. With air pollution being what it is today, it is really important to cleanse your skin. So this is the base you can continue with. Then a second product to replace the moisture your skin loses during the day.'

C: 'It doesn't sting?'

H: 'No, you'll see when I put it on your face. First of all we have to try making your skin more absorbent so that it retains moisture. It is better for your skin if we try to make it react normally again. (Applies preparation.) You'll certainly agree with me that it's a pleasant feeling on the skin, not burning at all, isn't it?'

C: 'Yes, it's nice.'

H: 'That's because this preparation is perfectly adapted to your present skin condition.'

C: 'But what about the cream I have at home? Can I still use it?'

H: 'Well, it's like this. These preparations are co-ordinated in their composition to try and normalize your skin. You have been using a moisturizer for years but your skin is lacking in moisture. I don't think it will do your skin any good to use that cream again. Of course it's up to you whether you want to improve your skin condition in relation to its moisture content.'

C: 'Of course, if this will help it to improve! Does it depend on the moisture, then?'

H: 'In your particular case, yes.'

C: 'And then will it become better?'

H: 'Yes, because at the moment your skin lacks moisture. With this cream we can try to build the moisture up again so that in the long term the skin remains moist enough. I have written down instructions on how to follow the treatment which you can read at home. At the top, I have made a reminder to both of us to repeat your skin test on your next visit — you come every four weeks anyway — and then we can see how your skin has reacted. If there is any reason why you can't come, just call me and we'll arrange another appointment. Enjoy yourself tonight!'

(For an analysis of this dialogue see pp. 108-109.)

Sales conversations that take place in car showrooms, or those of an industrial sales representative with his client, are somewhat similar.

INDUSTRIAL SALES REPRESENTATIVE

1. Appointment with customer — setting time and place.
2. Reception, greeting.
3. Enquiry about customer's satisfaction with machines he has been using up until now. Note down any complaints.
4. Be attentive to (product-relevant) problems and desires of customer (increased economy, capacity, reliability, facility in handling and ease of operation); agreement on needs and their relative importance;
5. Presentation of offer (graphs, technical drawings, photographs). Distribution of promotional material.
6. Point by point agreement between customer's needs and the offer is demonstrated and confirmed;
7. Possible invitation to demonstration in factory;
8. Final agreement with closing motivation;
9. Financial and other arrangements;
10. Delivery;
11. Follow-up conversations (in person or by telephone).

CAR SALESMAN

1. Enquiry by telephone or in person;
2. Reception.
3. Specification (customer's requirements: 2nd hand car, use, motive, consumer category).
4. Agreement on customer's requirements.
5. Presentation of offer by demonstration with stationary vehicle and on test drive. Coverage of needs and requirements through discussion, possibly distribution of promotional ma-

terial, minimizing short-comings;

6. Point by point agreement between customer's needs and the offer is demonstrated and confirmed;
7. Final agreement with closing motivation;
8. Financial and other arrangements;
9. Delivery;
10. Follow-up conversations (in person or by telephone).

PRACTICE EXAMPLE OF SALES QUESTIONING TECHNIQUE
(Please analyse using the table on page 112.)

Did you ever hear or have a conversation like this?

Scene: Car showroom.

— Good morning.
1. 'Good morning, my name is Miller. I see you are interested in sports cars, Mr. . . .?'
2. 'Sheen. Yes, a nice car. How much is it?'
3. 'Yes, Mr. Sheen, a beautiful car, our top model; with its 2,500 c.c. it does a good 120 M.P.H. What are you driving at the moment?'
4. 'An XYZ coupé. I've been very satisfied with it but now that it's three years old, it's starting to need repairs. How much do you think I could get for it?'
5. 'I'll call our second-hand car manager to give you a quote, rather than me giving you the wrong price . . . Do you have 20 or 30 minutes to spare, Mr. Sheen?
   Yes? Wonderful.
   (Second-hand car manager comes)
   Do you have the registration papers on you? Then we won't have to ask you for all the details. Thank you. How many miles have you done in the last three years?'
6. '55,000 miles.'
7. 'Oh, you're on the road quite a bit. Is it mainly cross-country or short distances, Mr. Sheen?'

8. 'Well, it's a mixture of both. In my job as industrial sales representative for heavy-duty machines I have to drive both long journeys and short distances in the city. I need a reliable car and I can't arrive feeling tired and worn out.'

9. 'Yes, when you have tiring negotiations relaxed driving is an absolute necessity. You don't carry a lot of luggage, do you?'

10. 'Travelling luggage for a maximum of one week plus my brief-case with papers and construction drawings.'

11. 'So you don't need a lot of extra space that you would only be driving around with you. Which of our models interests you the most?'

12. 'Your 900 models. They can accelerate to 100 M.P.H. within 11 seconds, can't they?'

13. 'We have two models. The smaller one needs a little over 11 seconds and the top model you chose straight away needs only 8 seconds. It also looks more like a sportscar and has a higher prestige value because of its overtaking potential. This means a higher average speed, but I don't have to tell that to an experienced driver like yourself. Which model do you think would help you to arrive at your destination feeling more relaxed, Mr. Sheen?'

14. 'Hm. With the same type of driving, surely the larger model. But don't you think it encourages speeding?'

15. 'Isn't that a question of character, Mr. Sheen? An experienced driver like yourself wouldn't be nearly as tempted as a novice, would he?'

16. 'Well . . .'

17. 'Our models also include the tempostat. Do you happen to know anything about it?'

18. 'Yes. Isn't it a kind of speed regulator?'

19. 'That's right, Mr. Sheen. If you set the tempostat at the desired speed, you can forget about the accelerator. Of course you can still accelerate when you like as well as brake, and when you release the brakes or the accelerator the car readjusts itself to the desired speed. Don't you think this would contribute to relaxed driving for a tired businessman?'

20. 'I'm sure it would. What's the price of this model?'

21. 'The standard model of this ABC 900 costs around $12,500. Surely this is the car you're looking for, don't you think, Mr. Sheen?'

22. 'Well, yes. But I didn't realize it would be so expensive.'

23. 'Don't you always hear that when you present your precision ma-

chines, Mr. Sheen? As an experienced businessman, it must be clear to you that quality products have their price . . .'

Did you notice how skillfully this salesman guided his customer. He did make some minor mistakes, but then nobody is perfect. He first asked the customer about his needs and requirements and his address was taken down. Questions were used in a variety of ways.

How much more elegant, pleasant, brief and to the point is a conversation that is guided by questioning rather than the one where argument is followed by objection and opinion by counter-opinion, as in the following excerpt from a conversation.

— 'Good morning.'
— 'Good morning. My name is Miller. I'm interested in buying a new car. (Pause) Isn't that an XYZ 900?'
— 'Yes, with 2,500 c.c. it does an easy 120. Especially attractive is the design with large window area giving optimum view. Rear-engined, of course, whereas the other models still have front engines.'
— 'Well, I did hear, and it was also written about in *Auto-Home* magazine, that your company also does a front-engined car now.'
— 'Well, that's possible, especially when you have to comply with regulations.' (Pause)
— 'I would like to have a look at the engine. That's a six cylinder, isn't it?'
— 'Yes, with an elevated camshaft, secure rotation, it accelerates from 0 to 100 in 9 seconds. Top performance!'

The sales consultant tries to direct his customer by questions. At the outset, he initiates the conversation through harmless opening questions to put the customer into the role of answerer, and not the other way round. By using questions that elicit answers, he secures for himself the role of consultant.

With the first information questions, he sets up the basic framework — what problem, product or need is being talked about. The limits of other possibilities are clarified. The opinions and interests of the customer in relation to specific details such as practical problems, special focal points, important motives and experiences are discovered. Through concluding questions, the salesman skillfully directs the attention of his conversation partner to points relevant to both where agreement can be reached between need and offer. In principle, this means 'making our own thoughts the thoughts of the other'.

As you have probably experienced, biting counter-arguments tend to inhibit the development of a conversation. Ultimately, they reach a dead end. Isn't it more profitable to ask a question about the reasons why in order to loosen up the opposition and to gain the partner's willingness to allow other points of view to come into play?

The meaning of questioning dialogue in a sales situation is to recognize the goal and to direct the conversation towards this goal, with every agreement being confirmed along the way by the partner.

11

THE CONSULTATION

Individual advice through questioning.

'Direct questions of a delicate nature should only be asked late in the conversation.' (Dührssen)

Who hasn't at some time been asked for advice? One suddenly finds oneself in the role of consultant, marriage counselor or careers advisor. The problems encountered in counseling are as diverse as life itself. The consultation is set up to deal with those areas of life experience where problems occur more frequently or at least prove difficult to solve; or to give advice on opportunities and alternatives in commercial situations. Here we would like to concentrate on social counseling.

COUNSELING

SOCIAL	ECONOMIC
educational	management
maternal	training
school	computer service
youth	industrial efficiency
marriage	tax
psycho-therapeutic	legal
vocational	
religious	
rehabilitation	
welfare	

Although the majority of counselors qualify for their profession through their educational or other achievements, the general bases of counseling are seldom clarified.

'Counseling' implies that a single course of action is not dictated to the individual seeking advice and that there is room for him to choose from different possibilities available, carrying out his decision independently. The key to counseling is that the individual seeks advice of his own free will. The goal of counseling consists in bringing a problem closer to its resolution. A counselor is not a problem solver but rather a catalyst through which an individual comes to know his problems better.

Feasible alternatives for action and decision-making should be made clear and accessible to the individual seeking advice.

The problems of every individual are unique. Whoever thinks that therefore each consultation runs a unique course with no common pattern or recognized system of characteristics confines himself to the role of confidant: in short, he doesn't need to understand anything, the main point being that the individual seeking advice express himself freely.

Nothing against freedom of expression, but something more is expected from a counseling centre, namely a diagnosis of the problem, a mirror of its causes and their inter-relation. A counselor relying only on information arising spontaneously and on random impressions will soon be lost when it comes to presenting decision-alternatives.

A counseling session is only possible if the individual seeking advice still relates consciously to his own experience, that is if he is not mentally ill. One should really expect him to be able to communicate freely his subjective experience of crucial periods in his life. In addition, the counseling session requires that the individual warm up quickly, dropping his defenses and inhibitions; often other problems are simulated, roles are played and lies are told. Experience shows that in many cases the client lacks the necessary ability and relaxation to articulate freely. This is where your help with questioning technique can begin. Here counseling becomes an interaction that is 'client-centered' (Carl Rogers) and a specific role is assigned to the counselor, 'who tries to understand emotional aspects of experience in verbal and non-verbal behaviour', reflecting back to the client what he has understood. What is reflected should not be experienced as threatening by the client.

Moreover, the counselor tries 'to transmit emotional warmth and positive regard to the other in such a way that he experiences the effort to understand as genuine concern.'[1]

A counselor should be:
— sensitive and open to the problems of others;
— sympathetic and rational in his approach to conflict situations;
— differentiating in his perception (not wanting to oversimplify);
— able to evaluate the realness of the problem, its displacements and repressions (for example, recognition of the often unconscious discrepancy between what an individual describes as his problem and what it is 'in reality').

In addition, a counselor should be aware of the imbalance of the conversation situation ('he knows something that I, the client, don't know'). It is primarily as a result of this imbalance that the counseling situation comes to exist in the first place. Another thing that every counselor should understand very clearly is that he will be held responsible for the success of the session. The individual seeking advice wants a recipe and he imagines the counselor's knowledge to be a recipe book. He doesn't realize that the objective is not to bake a new cake or to create a human being from a test tube, but rather to deal with a cake that didn't turn out. Neither the cook (client) nor the counselor know the ingredients used, or for how long or at what temperature (environmental influences) the cake has been baked.

The counseling situation can only be mastered if the client's own responsibility is made sufficiently clear to him. The aim of the counselor therefore consists in 'providing for the client full and responsible access to his own experiencing' and to offer practical alternatives. How can this be accomplished without the appropriate use of questioning techniques?

The following conversation structure is a product of the intentions of both partners, their roles and the conversation situation:

1. The individual seeking advice (client) adjusts himself to the (unknown for him) situation and the (unknown) conversation partner (counselor) and describes his case. (If he were sent by a court, he would tell his 'story' differently.) The case is the counselor's official assignment.

2. The counselor concentrates on structure, that is he tests his hypothesis about symptoms and causes against the story and therefore focuses mainly on these aspects. When material comes up that doesn't fit in with his theoretical knowledge, he probes further. By repeated changes in emphasis (the subordinate clauses of the client may become the main clauses of the counselor), he indicates how he views the problem (mostly neutral open information questions, partly confirmation questions). He defines 'the problem' by constant selection and combination of elements and expressions he considers significant. Possibly he sees the starting point for long-term counseling; e.g. instead of 'momentary assistance during a divorce procedure', perhaps 'intervention to avoid a divorce altogether'.

3. The counselor tries to clarify the client's description (open, non-suggestive questions and partly indirect questions where taboos must be overcome).

4. Analysis presented in the form of an interpretation. This will

not be in scientific jargon but will describe the 'situation defined' as it presents itself to the client.

5. The client's reaction should follow this analysis (limitation, contradiction, agreement) even if it has to be provoked (clarification of both points of view through neutral open questions).

6. Joint development of possible action and decisions (concluding, open questions), evaluation of alternatives (partly suggestive questions where inhibitions might preclude practical possibilities).

When dealing with objective situations, which appear socially neutral with few alternatives possible, — for instance in educational guidance, — it is sometimes simpler to ask closed questions.

For example: 'Do you also have a full-time job?'
'Does the child occasionally have fevered nightmares?'
'Is it the eldest of your children or a younger child?'

Generally, in the enquiry and clarification stage, open questions will be asked. The answers received are again questioned suggestively in the course of clarification to arrive at an evaluation.

For example (in marriage counseling): 'What is really important for you?'
'How important is it to live with a man who loves you in this way — a man whom you share with another woman?'
'How important is this partner for you and your family, given that he does not respond to any of your wishes (in so far as he is aware of them at all)?'
'How much do you need your partner?'
'Can't you do without him, despite all the hurt and pain?'

The central question: 'How do you *experience* . . . . . ?' If you omit this question from a consultation, then you are not really interested in the concerns of your client. It is not you who are called upon to evaluate and judge the problem, but the client. Only when you realize what all this means to him can you offer suggestions for a solution.

An important aspect of questioning technique is the use of impulses or stimuli. In the counseling situation this would involve describing how you as a human being experience a particular behaviour pattern or intention of the client. In this way, you are not expressing an official evaluation, nor making a reproach or an accusation, nevertheless the client is confronted and is challenged indirectly to make a statement.

The following is an example of marriage counseling.[2]

A married couple enters into counseling to avoid an impending divorce. Throughout the counseling sessions they quarrel continually, blaming each other for past incidents. Each defends his/her version of the truth tenaciously. Periodically they call upon the counselor to act as referee who, knowing only two contradictory versions, cannot solve the problem, let alone judge what it is about. Several times during these quarrels the wife, finding her husband's interpretation entirely false, introduces her responses with phrases such as, 'Now you are being silly . . .' or 'Now don't be silly!'. When the counselor wants to point out the 'alienating nature' of this form of communication and make the wife understand that by labelling her husband as 'of unsound mind' she is blocking resolution of the problem under discussion, he can present his observations in the following different forms.

He states his observation and asks the husband to express how he feels when he hears this phrase. He explains to the wife that she is moving onto another level with this phrase and that her husband's reaction can no longer be directed towards the topic itself. The counselor describes the impression the phrase, 'Don't be so silly' made upon him, saying that 'it left me feeling a bit helpless because you can hardly expect to solve problems with silly people. I had the impression you wanted to disarm your husband for any future undertaking.'

In the third reaction mode mentioned there are some important structural elements that need to be interpreted. The communication level shifts from the marriage partners to the counselor and the wife. The reaction mode repeats the content of the problem on a level that is emotionally different: the emotional reaction of the counselor is revealed and therefore makes him vulnerable. Both partners have an opportunity to contradict: the husband could say that it does not worry him in the least, which would soundly confuse the counselor in his strategy; or the wife could say (and she did in real life) that she hadn't even realized she used that expression several times and that in any case she behaved in a way totally different from what was perceived by the counselor.

A fourth mode of reaction of the counselor could be to set up a game situation where the problem would be discussed between the marriage partners, on condition that every contribution be introduced with phrases like, 'Oh, you are stupid!', 'It's impossible to talk with you' or 'That's nonsense!', etc.

In the first mode of reaction (reference questions to the husband), the counselor appears more as a neutral strategist, fruitfully arranging all future discussion. In the second mode of reaction (explanation to the wife), he appears more as an objective informer in that he is attempting to initiate a cognitive learning process. In the third mode of reaction, he makes an interpretation, as described above. In the fourth mode of reaction, he is a game-master who makes the rules and through that produces experiences.

Each of these modes of reaction is possible and valid. None can be dismissed as ineffectual although they are based on widely differing theoretical concepts which should be clear to the counselor if his mode of reaction deserves to be called a strategy.

REFERENCES

1. Speierer, G. W.: 'Gruppendynamik', 4/75.
2. Mader, W.: 'Alltagswissen, Diagnose, Deutung in Beratungssituationen', Zeitschrift für Padagogik, 1976.

12

QUESTION TIME!
TALK SHOWS AND
JOURNALISTIC INTERVIEWS

When a listener to radio or television interviews occasionally hears questions like, 'What does it feel like to win this sports trophy?' or 'What does it feel like to be reunited with your family after so many years of separation?', he feels sorry for the person being questioned and also for the questioner. It is only too obvious that these are emergency questions and that there was not enough time for preparation.

Even the most skillful questioning technique is no help if the interviewer doesn't know what he should be asking. Subject material, intention and questioning technique can be combined to create such fascinating conversations that a separate entertainment category has been created for them — the talk show: brilliant, carefully aimed questions on the one side, with charm, wit and humour on the other. That's real entertainment!

And what about the intention? To extract the innermost thoughts, opinions and plans from the individual questioned, to show surprising aspects of a personality who is always seen exclusively in the role of politician, movie-star or scientist. Alternatively, the intention may be to report objectively, without personal bias, particular circumstances and events. Up until recently insight into journalistic questioning techniques was gained primarily through practical experience and by studying brilliant examples. It was therefore regarded as an art rather than a skill. But certain basic skills should be not only theoretical but also applicable in practice:

— journalistic questions are in general sharply provocative, as they deal with negative developments and consequences;
— seemingly positive subject areas are questioned;
— the negative critical core contains a certain amount of truth and validity;
— as much as possible, all interesting aspects corresponding with the desires of the public are discussed;
— opposites are constructed and past successes or goals are presented in a more positive light;
— the choice of words is very colourful, often dramatic — there is no restraint. Not polite paraphrasing but well-directed comments about the topic are needed. Call a spade a spade.

The mechanism is clear:

• provocation, then follow up at weak points;
• provocative questions as well as questions exposing weak points are carefully prepared.

These questions almost always contain a provocative element, to the point of being models of suggestive questions. Indirect questions which lead the individual to accept assumptions that are true but cannot be talked about, and to answer on the basis of these assumptions, are especially useful. A favourite form of indirect questioning which is quite effective is to present a choice of alternatives from a wide range of possible answers. Although an information question is open, it also exerts a suggestive influence through its choice of words. Guidance by the interviewer is totally clear and therefore accepted.

The mechanism of hidden questions works in the sense that compromising questions are asked with a view to exposing the basis of the response elicited.

The journalist cannot help but construct certain hypotheses which he tests during the conversation. Knowing as much as possible about the person being interviewed enables the direction of the answers to be predictable to a certain extent (especially with politicians, lobbyists and representatives of institutions that have a specific programme). This knowledge allows indirect questions to be formulated in such a way that premises cannot be totally rejected and the question is still taken seriously. Here again, 'Anything goes'. Sophisticated formulation, incisive approach.

A few tips:

— show interest through: eye contact

taking notes

nodding the head

short throw-aways

but no value judgements;

— important to reduce tension with a brief introduction;

— make opening questions as wide as possible, gradually narrowing the focus to the direct question;

— 'why' questions are dangerous in an interview and should generally be avoided as the person being interviewed usually searches for reasons that are totally unrelated to his real motivation;

— if questioned directly, people have a general tendency to idealize aspects of their behaviour that involve a high degree of social approval/disapproval and that are closely connected to their self-image.

A brilliant example of journalistic questioning technique is shown in the following interview, 'We need atomic energy'.[1]

Reporter (R), Government Official (O)

R: 'In many parts of Germany, people have protested against the erection of nuclear power plants and the disposal of nuclear waste. Is this fear justified or is it irrational?'

O: 'A mixture of both. Obviously we are not dealing here with totally harmless technology. The question is, are the risks with nuclear energy any higher than those that are accepted without problem in other areas of industry and civilisation? In my opinion, the answer is no.'

R: 'Which particular areas do you have in mind?'

O: 'For example, through political and organizational decisions we could reduce the 14,800 deaths in traffic accidents annually to approximately 11,000. In 15 years, this would mean approximately 50,000 real and not just hypothetical lives saved.'

R: 'But the protesters are afraid that something much worse might happen. Is there any guarantee that security regulations are sufficient to prevent a nuclear disaster?'

O: 'Up until now, we have had no serious reactor accident anywhere through which innocent people could have been badly injured. The probability is very low and the risk, as I said, is in any case no greater than in other areas of technology.'

R: 'What about contamination by radiation?'

O: 'The ceiling levels authorized by the Federal Government are very low compared with other countries. We have estimated that in 1985 when something like 15% of our power needs will be met by atomic energy, contamination by radiation will be only one-fiftieth of what is caused at present by medical diagnosis.'

R: 'The central problem remains unsolved. What can we do about radioactive waste?'

O: 'It only remains unsolved in the sense that the necessary plants have not been constructed on a sufficiently large scale in this country. We have learned a great deal from disposal and recycling plants in America, England and France as well as from our own experimental plants, so that we are now in a position to present clear-cut solutions to this problem on a large scale.'

R: 'So the construction of nuclear power plants has advanced too rapidly in relation to the problem of waste disposal?'

O: 'The Minister for the Interior has stated, and I am in agreement with his opinion, that in future no authorization will be given to start production unless the problems of waste disposal and recycling have been resolved.'

R: 'Opponents of nuclear energy are much more willing to resort to legal proceedings than they were in the past to prevent the construction of nuclear power and disposal plants. Won't this delay the energy programme of the Federal Government?'

O: 'Up until now no damage has been done because, owing to the world-wide economic recession, the demand for electricity has in fact decreased. In the future, however, it would be useful if the electrical power industry would allow for extended time limits in their planning proposals so that court appeals can be settled in correct constitutional form.'

R: 'The demonstrators are concerned with the fundamental question: can we do without nuclear energy?'

O: 'Not if we want economic growth. And I think we must have growth as our entire economy is based on growth and expansion. We cannot take the risk of throwing our economy into chronic depression because an essential factor is missing.'

R: 'Couldn't this energy gap be met by exploitation of solar energy or wind energy?'

O: 'Even if we draw on energy sources such as the sun, wind and the heat of the earth, and we are already doing quite a lot in these areas, we still need nuclear energy.'

R: 'Are the demonstrators the machine breakers of the atomic age?'

O: 'Among the protesters against nuclear energy are not only those who want to stop nuclear energy at all costs. There are also intelligent environmentalists who want to emphasize through their protest the question: what kind of growth do we want to strive for in the years to come?'

R: 'Why do we need even more energy in the future?'

O: 'Because with increasing pressure through competition and probably also the higher costs of raw materials, we can only maintain full employment and our high standard of living if we can finance the investments necessary with real growth.'

R: 'The opponents may be willing to give that up. Should an opinion poll be conducted to find out what the people really want?'

O: 'Such referendums are not provided for in the constitution and I think with good reason. I would like to see a wide and far-reaching discussion on the overall problem: How do we want to live? What type of economic growth do we want to attain? How can we protect our environment more effectively? How can we use less raw materials? And finally, what industrial structure do we want to develop in order to remain competitive on the international market?'

REFERENCE

1. Interview translated from *Wirtschaftswoche* 48/76.

FIELDS OF APPLICATION OF QUESTIONING TECHNIQUE

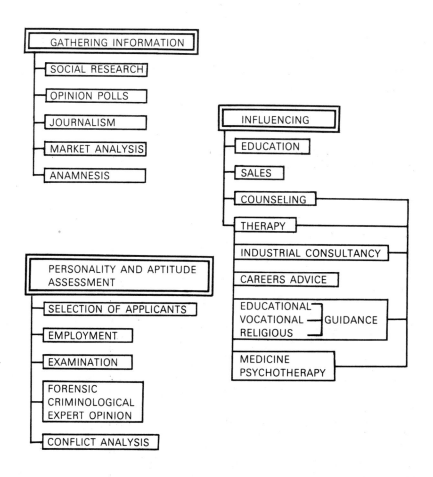

ANALYSIS OF THE STRUCTURE OF A SALES CONVERSATION WITH A NEW CUSTOMER

(See example on pp. 84-86.)

1. Customer makes appointment personally or by telephone. Questions about address, including telephone number (in case appointment changes), how customer found this salon, general wishes, entry onto card index system.

2. Reception (by manager/manageress or assistant), creating an informal atmosphere.

3. Questions about type of hair-style, what has client been doing up until now for hair, skin and body care (which enables us to learn about needs, expectations, financial commitment and attitude), acknowledge that client has shown interest in taking care.

4. Evaluation of present condition from customer's point of view.

5. Diagnosis by skilled assistant/manager.

6. Agreement about condition and evaluation between customer and assistant/manager (the basis of all future action, therefore agreement about needs and requirements is an absolute must!). Possible consequences of present treatment may be mentioned.

7. Agreement on aim.

8. Stepwise description of the treatment. Complete prescription for the aim agreed upon, in view of past financial commitment (see point 3.). Give reasons for particular prescription, explaining purpose of preparation and its effects. Indicate that initial treatment will be with less-concentrated preparations. Adjust prescription frequently according to changes in skin condition. (While prescribing you are on the same level as the customer.)

9. Demonstration: showing the preparation to the customer; demonstration of use with description.

10. Warn customer about possible side-effects (smell, initial scaling).

11. After treatment, closing motivation ('beautiful'), giving copy of prescription with instructions for application.

12. Arrange for check-up appointment.

QUESTION TYPE AND FUNCTION
ACCORDING TO THE DIFFERENT PHASES

QUESTION TYPES				QUESTION
Open/ Closed	*Direct/ Indirect*	*Suggestive/ Non-suggestive*	*Hidden/ Clear*	**FUNCTION**
open	direct	non-suggestive	clear	information questions
open	direct	partially suggestive	clear	opening and personal questions
open, later possibly closed	direct and indirect	non suggestive to suggestive	clear	information questions; in the case of assumptions — confirmation
open if dissatisfaction clear; closed if doubtful	direct	to suggestive	clear	information questions; in the case of assumptions — confirmation
mostly closed, sometimes open	direct	non-suggestive	clear	information questions; in the case of assumptions — confirmation
closed	direct to indirect	suggestive	clear	confirmation and agreement; perhaps concluding questions
closed	direct	suggestive	clear	confirmation
open to closed	direct to indirect	non-suggestive to suggestive	clear	concluding, confirmation and decision questions
open to closed	direct	non-suggestive	clear	checking questions
closed to open	direct	suggestive	clear	confirmation
closed to open	indirect	suggestive to non-suggestive	clear	agreement

TABLE FOR ANALYSIS OF PRACTICE EXAMPLES:

Conversation Phase:

Correct / Incorrect	Open / Closed	Direct / Indirect	Suggestive / Non-suggestive	Hidden / Clear

TABLE FOR ANALYSIS OF PRACTICE EXAMPLES:

Conversation Phase:

Correct/ Incorrect	Open/ Closed	Direct/ Indirect	Suggestive/ Non-suggestive	Hidden/ Clear

TABLE FOR ANALYSIS OF PRACTICE EXAMPLES:

Conversation Phase:

Correct/ Incorrect	Open/ Closed	Direct/ Indirect	Suggestive/ Non-suggestive	Hidden/ Clear

BIBLIOGRAPHY

Arbeitsgruppe Information: 'Kommunikation', 1974.

Aretz, N.: 'Fahrplan für das Einstellungsinterview', Plus 6/72.

Beiner, F.: 'Studientext zur Formulierung von Prüfungsleistungen', 1976.

Berne, E.: 'Games People Play', 1964.

Bloom, B. S.: 'Taxonomy of Educational Objectives' Vol. 1.

Blum, M. L.: 'Industrial Psychology', 1968.

Döring, V. W.: 'Prüfungsmethode und Prufungspsychologie', unveroffentlichte Seminarunterlage 1976.

Dührssen, A.: 'Psychotherapie bei Kindern und Jugendlichen', 1960.

Feldmann, P.: 'Verkaufstraining', 1973.

Flechsig, K. H.: 'Prüfungen und Evaluation', 1974.

Harris, T. H.: 'I'm OK — You're OK', 1969.

Hornstein, W.: 'Beratung in der Erziehung', Zeitschrift für Padagogik, 5/75.

Kaiser, A.: 'Druck erzeugt Gegendruck', 1975.

Kaiser, A.: 'Erfolgreich lehren in Aus- und Fort-bildung' 1976.

Katona, G.: 'Psychological Economics', 1975.

Knebel, H.: 'Das Vorstellungsgesprach', 1972.

König, R.: 'Das Interview', 1965.

Mader, W.: 'Alltagswissen, Diagnose, Deutung in Beratungs situationen', Zeitschrift für Padagogik, 5/76.

Meininger, J.: 'Success through Transactional Analysis', 1955.

Neuberger, O.: 'Das Mitarbeitergespräch', 1973.

Rogers, C. R.: 'Client-Centered Therapy', 1951

Schraml, W.: 'Das psychodiagnostische Gespräch', Handbuch der Psychologie, Volume 6, 1964.

Speierer, G. W.: 'Gruppendynamik', 4/75.

Stangl, A. & M. L.: 'Verhandlungsstrategie', 1972.

Weidenmann: 'Fragen' in 'Reden und reden lassen', 1975.